Praise for

MASTER YOUR CASH FLOW

"With the abundance of financial books, blogs, courses, and apps in the marketplace, Albert Zdenek, Jr. cuts through the clutter by giving you a cohesive and integrated financial strategy to take control of your financial life. Chapter by chapter, it outlines how to grow and retain wealth by making better choices, overcoming obstacles, and understanding the financial tools. Bottom line, the book helps lead the reader toward wealth creation, sustainability, and financial independence. Read it!"

—Pam Laudenslager, two-time Tony Award-winning Broadway producer; president, Hemisphere Two Entertainment, LLC

"I have known and worked with Al and his team for the best part of ten years; their passion and dedication for their clients always inspires me. This book is a valuable tool for all individuals, executives, and business owners. It has provided me and my family with a simple and straight-forward disciplined process to make smarter financial decisions and transform our lives. Using the "Wealth Building Formula®" is now part of my life, and the results have been invaluable."

—Patrick D.C. Williams, CEO, The Thursday Room; former publisher, *Worth Magazine*

"I tell everyone that next to my wife, meeting Al Zdenek was the most important thing to happen in my life. Prior to working with Al, my retirement savings consisted solely of an IRA contribution of $2,000 per year and a monthly whole-life premium. Al provided direction, structure, and encouragement for a lifetime savings strategy that guarantees that I will retire on time and with the wealth I need for years to come while living the way I want now. More than telling me what I should do, Al *taught me* how to make better financial decisions and invest wisely and for the long term. This book contains the insights that transformed my life and will help everyone to realize that living the way you wish now, building wealth and retiring when you wish are absolutely within reach. As Al says, retirement is not the day you stop working, it is the day you have the freedom to decide what *you want to do* with the rest of your life."

—Hershey S. Bell, MD, MS, FAAFP; professor, vice president for academic affairs, and dean, LECOM School of Pharmacy

"Simply put, my wife and I, like most couples, have completely different views on how to spend money, save for retirement, and manage our current cash flow. Even though we make plenty of money, we just come from a difference place. After reading *Master Your Cash Flow*, we engaged Al Zdenek as our wealth advisor. Al helped us implement the Wealth Building Formula® offered in the book. He helped both my wife and I gain clarity around how to live the life we wanted now and our vision for the future and see exactly what we need to do to achieve that vision. Surprisingly, it's a lot easier than we could have imagined. I wish we could have gained this knowledge years ago."

—David Zelman, Ph.D.; founder and president, Transitions Institute, Inc.; author, *If I Can, You Can*

"I've had the good fortune of knowing Al Zdenek for over thirty-five years. During that time, observing and participating in the evolution of Al's thinking and development of the technical concepts of financial planning has been inspiring and personally rewarding. Al was at the forefront of addressing an unmet need for his clients at a time when few professionals understood the demand for a holistic approach to achieving financial independence. The thesis and direction Al provides in this book has been tested by the fire of the 2008 crash and recession. His results with his clients are a testament to the successful paradigm Al describes for achieving not only financial security but also one's lifetime goals."

—William H. Koster, Ph.D., former EVP, R&D, Bristol-Myers Squibb; CEO, Neurogen Corp.; currently President and CEO; Northern Pilot Co., LLC

"The concepts expressed in *Master Your Cash Flow* by author Al Zdenek have been life changing to me. Working hard and making a good living are classic American values. How to make better financial decisions, save and invest the money you make to reach a predetermined financial result is what is as important. Planning your financial future with the suggestions expressed in this book gives you immense power over how you design your future and enjoy the passage, living the life you want now. I suggest implementing these lessons to all the people I speak to about personal financial planning including all my business partners and my kids."

—Charles A. Accurso, M.D., FACG; founder and CEO, Digestive Healthcare Center & Central Jersey Ambulatory Surgical Center

"*Master Your Cash Flow* is a book that should be read by everyone the day before they receive their first paycheck. Nothing happens without a plan, and our financial security cannot be left to chance. Having the benefit of the lessons in this book through my personal experience with Al has given our family an understanding of the savings we have achieved, the best use of our earned income, and security about our retirement years ahead. Oh, how I wish I knew this forty years ago! We recently introduced Al to our six children (in their twenties) for a 'financial planning day.' They have begun to employ the concepts in this book, and my wish is that their early indoctrination will help them live a life of greater financial security."

—Bruce Raiffe, president, GUND

"Each story in this book provides a real-world example of the importance of finding ways to continually focus on being the *Master of Your Cash Flow*. I believe the key to living the life you want now and in the future is to make better financial choices, which most of us do not either have the time or knowledge to do. With practical solutions and real-world examples, Al Zdenek has shown how everyone can achieve their financial success and lifestyle by consistently making the right financial choices to accumulate wealth and to transform your life. The book empowers you to take control of your future without giving up the lifestyle you want to live today."

—Andrew Putterman, CEO, 1812Park, LLC; former CEO, Fortigent, LLC; former president, Lydian Wealth Management; former managing director head, HNW Strategies—LPL Financial

"Creating Wealth is *really* an accessible choice for all of us! Regardless of where you are starting, the journey of *Master Your Cash Flow* will guide you step by step through the process of financial transformation through the trusting voice and experience of Al Zdenek. Financial growth requires taking risks and making changes. The challenge for each of us is charting the right path forward . . . this book helps you to customize your personal roadmap!"

—Erica Peitler, leadership performance coach;

author, *Leadership Rigor* and *Open Up and Say aaah!*

"*Master Your Cash Flow* is a must-read by anyone interested in managing their financial future. Al Zdenek uses his years of entrepreneurial, financial, and investment experiences to give the reader real advice and empower them to grow their wealth and to live the life they desire now and in the future. The pages of this book guide and educate the reader in practical and easy-to-read language on the process to create a financial plan and then execute against that plan for future financial well-being. I too frequently have seen very successful entrepreneurs and business leaders not pay attention to financial planning and wealth management only to find out that the plan they had in their head was only a wish. Plan your life and personal finances like you plan your business. In *Master Your Cash Flow,* Al Zdenek provides you the methodology to do just that. A most important, great book to read!"

—Lee Froschheiser, executive chairman and senior consultant, Management
Action Programs, Inc.; author, *Vital Factors: The Secret to Transforming Your Life*

MASTER YOUR CASH FLOW

MASTER YOUR CASH FLOW

THE KEY TO GROW AND RETAIN WEALTH

Albert J. Zdenek, Jr., CPA/PFS

Published by Advantage, Charleston, South Carolina.
Member of Advantage Media Group.

ADVANTAGE is a registered trademark and the Advantage colophon is a trademark of Advantage Media Group, Inc.

Printed in the United States of America.

ISBN: 978-1-59932-713-6
LCCN: 2016932551

This publication is designed to provide accurate and authoritative information in regard to the subject matter covered. It is sold with the understanding that the publisher is not engaged in rendering legal, accounting, or other professional services. If legal advice or other expert assistance is required, the services of a competent professional person should be sought.

Advantage Media Group is proud to be a part of the Tree Neutral® program. Tree Neutral offsets the number of trees consumed in the production and printing of this book by taking proactive steps such as planting trees in direct proportion to the number of trees used to print books. To learn more about Tree Neutral, please visit **www.treeneutral.com**. To learn more about Advantage's commitment to being a responsible steward of the environment, please visit **www.advantagefamily.com/green**

To Dad, who taught me patience,
dedication to work, sacrifice for and loyalty to family,
and to laugh and enjoy life along the way.

Table of Contents

Introduction 1

CHAPTER ONE
Making Better Financial Choices —
Determining How You Wish to Live Your Life 7

CHAPTER TWO
The Obstacles 21

CHAPTER THREE
Becoming the Master of Your Cash Flow 31

CHAPTER FOUR
The Wealth Building Formula® 47

CHAPTER FIVE
The Power of Compounding 57

CHAPTER SIX
The Tax Saving Savings Effect 67

CHAPTER SEVEN
Finding More Investable Cash —Imagination 77

CHAPTER EIGHT
Using Debt Smarter —
the Truth about Debt and Wealth Creation 85

CHAPTER NINE
Other Ways to Find Investable Cash 99

CHAPTER TEN

What Being a Savvy Investor Really Means —Knowing Your
Long-Term Investment Return Objective 111

CHAPTER ELEVEN

Estate Planning —Protecting What You Have Built 123

CHAPTER TWELVE

Creating a Championship Team 129

In Closing 135
Contact Information 137
About the Author 139

Introduction

WHY I CHOSE TO
TRANSFORM LIVES

I call myself an accidental CPA. I went to college to be a geologist, but thanks to what was supposed to have been a side job in college, I discovered my true vocation: sophisticated tax planning for high-net worth individuals, families, corporate executives, and family-owned businesses. I rose to district manager of a tax preparation company. I was one of the youngest district managers they'd ever had. I started out with six offices and about two hundred employees and eventually expanded to ten offices. Gaining that familiarity with running a business was invaluable.

That experience convinced me that I needed to become a CPA because I loved tax work. Eventually, I earned my masters and worked in the tax department at Arthur Young & Company, one of the Big Eight accounting firms, in New York City. I loved working there and subsequently for Merck & Co. Inc. in the corporate tax department, but once you've run a business and called the shots, it's tough to work for someone else.

I started my own accounting firm in 1982. Within five years, my company had expanded to twenty-two employees and four partners. Even though I had a business to run, I had energy to spare, so I got involved with real estate investment on the side—to the tune of tens of millions of dollars. I also got involved in politics; I became a councilman and eventually the police commissioner of my town. If I had a spare hour during any week, I'd do something to fill it.

This all came crashing down for me in the mid to late 1980s when there was a recession. Quite frankly, I had my head handed to me; I had to lay off one-third of my company in a day. I had always been successful, and this was the first time in my life when I was failing. That was due to the cumulative effect of poor financial decisions, although I did not know that at the time. Because I'm a high-energy person, I started to look for ways to make up for some of the cash flow the business had lost due to the recession. I looked at personal financial planning, which was in its infancy then. There was no such thing as wealth management at that time. I started financial planning as another way to bring in income for my company, but I really did not know how to provide that service. Meanwhile, I had to give back real estate to the banks or sell it; it was a long process. I was determined to get through this, but I was worried: Was I going to work like this for the rest of my life? Would I be able to educate my children? Could I retire someday?

That's when I met some planners who actually showed me how to create my own financial plan—an idea that was completely foreign to me at that point. My clients always came first . . . I would get around to me someday. Now, seeing how financial planning worked for me, how it changed my life, I really wanted to learn how to provide it to others.

I worked in a bakery for thirteen summers as I was growing up. Being in a blue-collar family, I was taught that you work until sixty-five, and if you can retire then, fine. If not, you kept on working—and I worked with a lot of seventy- and eighty-year-old bakers. When I saw things crashing around me, I thought to myself, *Wow. Am I going to work like that for the rest of my life?*

When I started to provide financial planning for clients and saw how it transformed their lives, I became a real zealot. I could never transform a person's life with a better tax return but I could with financial planning and by helping him or her make better financial choices. It's simply poor financial decisions that keep people from achieving what they wish for in life now and in the future. When I ran my numbers, I saw what bad shape I was really in. But between my tax skills and what I had learned from the planners, I was able to put together a financial plan for myself with a goal to be financially independent by fifty—a goal I achieved when I was forty-eight.

It was just a question of making better financial decisions; most people don't realize that sometimes the smallest choice, such as whether you should lease or buy a car, can be a multimillion-dollar decision over time. This experience and the realization that I could transform lives by allowing people to live the lifestyles they wished to live now and still be able to retire and/or be financially independent in the time frame they chose thrilled me. I'm living proof of that—so are my clients.

I live in New York City and have a terrific apartment in Paris. I have a great company, work with a terrific team, and live a privileged lifestyle. It's not by accident; anyone can achieve this, if that's what they wish. I have taken people from having very little to financial independence: living the life they want and preserving and managing their wealth to make sure that they'll be able to do so for the rest of their lives. I still wake up every day excited by and looking forward to helping another person make better financial choices—transforming their lives.

Where to begin? I believe in having ground rules on how to work together, and I'd like to share with you the rules for reading this book.

THE GROUND RULES FOR SUCCESS

THIS BOOK IS NOT GOING TO ANSWER ALL YOUR QUESTIONS.

It's meant to give you an impetus to start asking them. It's meant to guide you and educate you. I may recommend things, but ultimately, you make all the decisions. No one is going to do this for you. This is your plan; this is your money. No one is going to have more interest in your money than you. To succeed in getting where you want to go, you'll need to create a financial plan and a road map to guide you toward achieving your goals. This book will help you:

- make better financial choices,
- reduce any personal-finance-related frustration or stress you may have in your life,
- achieve financial independence in a time frame that is reasonable for you, and
- if financially independent, preserve wealth while continuing to build new wealth.

Your financial plan will serve as the starting point of your action plan aimed toward achieving your desired financial goals. It will be a reference point from which you'll be able to review your progress each year and ensure that you are on the right track to achieving your financial-planning goals.

THIS IS YOUR FINANCIAL PLAN, AND YOU MUST PARTICIPATE IN IT.

Yes, you will need an expert team—and we'll get into what kinds of skilled players you'll need later on in this book—but no team and no advisor can make your decisions for you. This must be *your* plan because these are *your* goals, and ultimately what's affected is how *you* live now and in *your* future. Don't hand the reins to anyone. Your Wealth Building Formula® and road map will serve as guides in letting you know exactly where you are on this journey. The journey may seem to go slowly at first, but keep in mind that this is a marathon, not a sprint. Pay attention, ask questions, and take an active role.

PAST DECISIONS—LET THEM GO

In my experience, people come to us having made some excellent financial decisions and some poor financial decisions. I understand that you might feel some regret and embarrassment over past mistakes, but we're not here to focus on them. This book is here to help you make better financial choices going *forward* that are aligned with your financial and lifestyle goals.

WHAT ARE THE RESPONSIBILITIES OF THIS BOOK?

To answer as many of the potential questions you may have, as clearly as I can; to give you a process for making better financial choices; to give you clarity regarding concepts like making cash-flow management decisions like a well-run business; and to inspire you to achieve the financial life you wish to lead now and in the future.

CHAPTER ONE

MAKING BETTER FINANCIAL CHOICES—DETERMINING HOW YOU WISH TO LIVE YOUR LIFE

Life is the sum of all of your choices.
—Albert Camus

How do people make financial choices? Often they don't do so as well as they need to, largely because they're poorly informed about the impact of the choices they're making. It's not surprising; sadly, financial education in our country is nearly nonexistent. You're not taught finance in high school. You're taught history, math, and languages, but there's no course in which it's mandatory for you to understand how to balance your checkbook, how to apply for a car loan or a credit card, or how to save money, much less how to plan for your retirement. A physician once asked me what a CD was! He sheepishly said that he'd heard about these things that banks offered, but he didn't know what they were. This is a man who was a successful specialist and was renowned in his field, but somehow his extensive education hadn't included an explanation of what a certificate of deposit was.

Typically, when people go into their first job, their employer asks them if they want to participate in the company's 401(k). The new hire nods but is most likely thinking, "What is a 401(k)?" or, "Why do I need it?" They have no idea what a 401(k) is versus an IRA (individual retirement account). Added to that is the fact that as a consumer-oriented society, we're drilled with the idea that, "Okay, you've just gone through four years of study to get a college education. You deserve a really nice car and a wallet full of credit cards." Young (and some not-so-young) people make the mistake of taking on a lot of debt when they're least able to handle it.

By the way, I work with some of the smartest people around— physicians, attorneys, CPAs, business owners, and CEOs of major corporations—and they all have this same problem. They become masters at what they do, whether that's running a medical practice, an accounting firm, a law firm, their own business, or a major corporation, but when it comes to their personal financial lives, they haven't the faintest idea how to manage their personal cash flow. A CEO once told me, "I just got back from seeing my tax accountant. She told me that I earned almost $1 million last year. I was stunned. I asked her, 'Where did it all go?'" Yes, this CEO is a master of her profession, but she's not a master of her cash flow.

The fact is, if you want to create the life that you want now and in the future, you have to become the master of your cash flow— you need to understand some basics of finance and to learn to make better financial choices.

HOW DO YOU MAKE A BETTER CHOICE?

The answer to that question begins with another question: What kind of lifestyle do you wish to live *now*? There is a certain amount of cash flow that, if you had it coming in right now and for the rest of your life, inflation adjusted, would allow you to live the lifestyle you wanted to now and would make you financially independent. Discovering that number is the first thing on which to focus. This will lead to discovering the amount of wealth you need to accumulate or to preserve and manage.

There are a lot of "experts" who will tell you that you can figure this out on your own—maybe just by reading their book, taking a course, or putting your numbers in a software program. While figures can be calculated, the choices you make to accumulate wealth or to preserve and manage it are much more complex. For example, I know one person who just joined an exclusive organization of high-net worth members who look at how to invest and review investment opportunities every month. After eight months and eight one-day meetings, she told me, "I have learned so much. I now know how I want to invest my money." While I am sure she learned a good deal more than she had previously known, it isn't that simple. The effect of financial choices regarding cash flow, debt, taxes, insurance, estate planning, investing, and other financial aspects of one's life is much more complicated than that. Making the wrong choices can ensure that you work longer in life, leave you with less wealth and cash flow, or increase the risk in your investment portfolio.

It's natural for people who are masters in their own professions or businesses to assume that they can easily master the complexities of portfolio investment. They think that they can read a book, read the financial pages, follow a TV show, and more or less "visit" their money once every month or three and become as expert at managing it as people who do this as their profession, 24/7. How realistic is this?

Let's say that you wanted to master the game of tennis. If you play tennis one day a year, I doubt that you'd play very well. Maybe you think to yourself, *I'd improve if I played tennis once a month.* You might progress a little bit but probably not a lot. But you're determined to master this, so you decide to play tennis three times a week. Granted, you're probably never going to be Federer or Williams, but you know what? You'll play tennis a lot better with that constant practice than you would have if you did it once a year or once a month.

So could you do better if you became more involved with your portfolio? Sure. But as Benjamin Graham, Warren Buffet's mentor and the author of the iconic book *The Intelligent Investor*, suggested, to achieve good returns is not hard if you are willing to spend the time, but to achieve superior returns is harder than it looks. It is tough to do unless you are doing this 24/7.

Yet this is exactly what people do regarding their finances; a lot of very bright people get medical degrees, law degrees, accounting degrees, or financial degrees or establish successful companies, and because they're experts in their respective arenas, they assume that they can "visit" the investment management area or other areas of finance and know all there is to know about it.

I once jokingly asked a surgeon, "Can I take a course for a few days, read a book, or watch a series on TV and then go and do heart surgery?" Obviously not; you need to respect the fact that there are people who do their kind of work all day, every day, and are masters at it, whether it's in insurance, banking, accounting, estate work, or investment portfolio management. You cannot become an expert in all these areas, but you can surround yourself with experts who are equipped to help you make better financial choices.

I've given many lectures before groups of physicians who have just finished their residency programs and of other young professionals and executives just starting out their careers.

I start my speeches this way: "I see you all in my office in about twenty years, when you've really screwed up or you've made bad financial choices around debt, investments, or other financial matters. You're in your late forties or early fifties, and suddenly sixty doesn't look that far away, and now you're scared. Then you come to me so that we can start to set things right." I tell them that I'm there today to help them learn how to avoid some of those mistakes. That way, while they still may need some help, they're going to be in better financial shape in ten, twenty, or thirty years.

But it's important to understand that making better financial choices is not something you can visit once in a while or learn to do simply by reading a book (even this one) or by taking a course. Again, your best bet is to surround yourself with people who are going to help guide you on making better financial choices around a financial plan that lays out the way you want to live now and in the future.

Do you want less stress and anxiety? Do you know how much you have to save? Is the wealth you have now, plus what you're going to add to it, going to be enough? What is the average annual rate of return (what we call your long-term investment return objective) you need from your investment portfolio that makes everything work? Is your wealth protected?

Is your tax accountant calling you up before the end of the year to work up a tax projection of what your year looks like? She had better be because once the calendar year ends, nothing can be done. Or does your accountant just call you up on April 14th to inform you that you owe a lot of money . . . tomorrow? Possibly you didn't get your information in to your accountant until February, March, or April. You were too busy, and she is used to you being late anyway and just views your situation as tax work. In this case, your accountant is not helping you make better financial choices, find more cash flow, or build a financial future.

EVEN IF YOU'RE ALREADY FINANCIALLY INDEPENDENT, YOU NEED TO KNOW HOW MONEY WORKS

There is a great article in the December 15, 2015 issue of the *New York Times*: "Reversal of Fortunes for Some Superrich" (page B4). Just because you are rich doesn't mean you can't lose your wealth. If you're one of those very fortunate people who have the wealth to live the way they want now, it's important to make sure you can preserve and manage that wealth so that, in the future, you don't lose it because of poor financial decisions. You may be living a great lifestyle, but you wonder if you can sustain it or improve upon it.

I often work with high-net worth individuals; one example is a couple I met back in the nineties who had about ten million dollars' worth of real estate from which they were getting dependable rental income cash flow. They lived pretty simple lives and weren't outlandish in their spending. But there was an unanticipated change in the economy in their area, and all of a sudden there were vacancies in their buildings, which meant that their cash flow suddenly shrank. Even though they owned all of their real estate free and clear, without debt, instead of it making positive cash flow, they were now paying for their holdings out of pocket. Why? They still had to pay for maintenance, real estate taxes, and other operational expenses, all of which cut deeply into their income just as they were approaching retirement age.

Not surprisingly, at that point they panicked; they made some bad choices and got behind on their real estate taxes. Suddenly they were looking at a scenario in which they'd be forced to sell their properties in a down market, which would put them into a downward financial spiral of less and less income. They were trapped and didn't know which way to turn. That was the point at which they sought me out.

HOW CAN YOU FIX BROKEN CASH FLOW?

What poor financial choices had this couple made that brought them to this point? Certainly, somewhere along the line they could have made sure that they had significant cash reserves or had diversified into asset classes other than real estate. They could have sold off some of that real estate when the market was high and gotten into those other investments then so, when that got hit, they were not so badly affected.

Another mistake they made was one that most people make: they wanted to be out of debt by the time they retired. To them, having no debt was a sign of being successful. If you were in debt when you retired, you had to have failed at something. When the market changed, they weren't getting the same cash flow out of their properties. If they approached a bank to get a loan to cover some of the shortfall, what was the bank likely to do? A bank is only going to be your friend in good times; a bank is not there to take on risk and will only give you loans if you have adequate cash flow. Banks only give you money when you don't need them. This couple couldn't get loans from banks because even though they had the assets, they did not have the cash flow. They'd put all their eggs in one basket—and then dropped the basket.

What was I able to do? We looked at what they had and what they'd have to do with their properties to get themselves out of this situation. There were some properties they owned that, even in good times, weren't good cash flow producers, but they'd held on to them for personal reasons. That kind of thinking isn't helpful when you're trying to build cash flow. Bad real estate is like a bad stock. When the market goes down, if you're in a bad stock, you'd better sell it. If you're in a good stock, good stocks normally come back, just as good real estate normally comes back. Bad real estate and bad stocks do not, so there was some real estate they had to let go. When they did that, their cash flow improved because they were not stuck throwing money at bad properties. When their cash flow improved, we were able to go to a bank and show the bank that they were taking steps to improve cash flow. The bank decided that now they were a better risk, so it gave them some short-term borrowing ability. The borrowing allowed them to fix up properties to attract better tenants and to pay their expenses, so they didn't lose the buildings.

Then, as the market improved, they were able to take some of the excess cash flow, pay off their debt, and finally diversify into other assets. Even though it took a few years and they weren't able to keep all their property, the property and investments they had left were good, and they were able to produce the cash flow they required. They got to live the lifestyle they wished and secured that cash flow for the rest of their lives.

Another example of how you can fix broken cash flow even late in the game was a client of mine who was the former CEO of a Fortune 500 company. He had been retired for about ten years and was in his late seventies, approaching eighty. He was badly hit in a stock market crash because the investment holdings in his portfolio weren't sufficiently diversified. He had always had adequate cash flow before, so he and his wife had never really paid that much attention to their portfolio. Now they had to because their wealth was down quite a lot and was greatly affecting their cash flow. Mind you, these are people who had a penthouse, had helped found some very prominent charities, and were used to traveling to Europe every year. But as he was approaching eighty, they went on what I call a "survivor budget." They had pared down their life so much that they could not even participate in the charities that they'd founded. They scrapped the trip to Europe. Their penthouse had deferred maintenance on it because they couldn't afford to fix it up. As with most people who don't plan their finances properly or make poor financial choices, cash flow can seem to be all right in early retirement years but can suddenly become very tight when they're in their seventies and eighties—and it was becoming very tight for this couple. He was scared because his wife was younger, her mother was still alive, and his wife could easily live another twenty or thirty years. He was concerned about what to do.

I looked at his cash flow calculation very carefully and said, "I think you've made a mistake." He was concerned that he'd made a mistake with his numbers. I said, "I think you're a little short on your cash flow."

He said to me, "What do you mean?"

I said, "Well, don't you want to live the way you did before? Don't you want to travel to Europe? Don't you want to again participate in your charities? Don't you want to fix up this apartment and make sure at the same time your wife is going to be able to be financially independent beyond your own passing?"

He looked at me and said, "If you could do that, that would be wonderful." We looked at how he was structured around his taxes, his portfolio, and his debt, and we brought some better financial choices to what he was doing. With better choices, we were able to return him to the cash flow that allowed him to live the lifestyle he wanted to but also assured that his wife could continue to live in that same fashion, even if she lived to be one hundred. It is nearly never too late to correct poor choices to improve one's cash flow and financial condition. Doing so for this couple transformed their lives.

DON'T SET OUT WITHOUT A MAP

Of course, it's a lot easier to solve financial problems before they happen. It's analogous to taking a road trip. If you decide, "I'm in New York City, and I want to go to Oshkosh, Wisconsin," you can get in your car without any planning and just start traveling northwest on the highways that seem to be going in that direction— and hopefully, you'll get there somewhat in the time frame you wanted. Alternately, you could get yourself a reliable map, research the trip online, or consult a travel agent and plan your trip, including where to stop overnight, so that you know where you are at all times, can check your progress daily, and arrive at the time you wish and in the condition you wish.

A good financial plan is like that; it lets you say, "There's a goal I have in mind, but there's a preferred route I'd like to travel along on the way toward that goal—one that guarantees I'll get there in the manner I wish and be safe along the way." If you can do that, it greatly decreases the stress and anxiety you'll experience along the way. When life throws surprises at you, you'll be better able to handle them. Have you ever started out on a road trip only to discover that one of the major interstates is closed by an accident? If you have a good map, you can quickly find an alternate route. That's all this is. Sometimes people make seemingly random choices or quick decisions because they're busy and want to get it out of the way, but they'll put the time into planning a vacation, for instance, because that's more immediately enjoyable. That's the difference between someone making good financial choices and someone that sets himself up for potentially making bad financial choices.

WHAT WE DON'T KNOW CAN HURT US

Again, it comes down to how people are taught to make financial choices. We're usually taught in a few ways, but our first teachers are likely to be our parents. When we're first out into the adult world and need advice, we'll ask Mom or Dad, "How did you handle that?" We may start doing the same things our parents did. We may ask an older brother, sister, or friend; listen to pundits on TV; or read articles. We don't stop to think that the content in the article is generalized enough to apply to the masses; somehow we think that it's customized to us. Ultimately we make our choices the way others tell us to or based on how we've seen them make their choices. We don't judge whether they've been good or bad at it.

We wouldn't do this in other spheres: When you're really ill and you go to a physician, you're putting your trust in their hands to guide you past that illness. Unfortunately, perhaps, poor financial "health" doesn't always alert us with recognizable symptoms in the way that poor physical health usually does; often the effects of our poor financial choices creep up on us over a long period. We don't see the financial illness show up for twenty, thirty, or forty years, until finally we're in our fifties, sixties, or more likely our seventies. Now, cash flow is getting tight, and we can't afford certain things because we didn't realize that the decisions we made thirty or forty years ago would affect us in the ways they do today.

If someone were on fire, their response would be immediate: they would jump up and down and scream in pain, right? When a financial professional like me sees you making poor financial choices, it is like seeing you on fire, except you are not jumping up and down and screaming. You are just sitting there, burning, maybe even pouring on more gas by making more poor financial choices. When it's a "financial fire," people don't feel the burn, so they just keep on going as they have been. If you have an infected appendix and choose not to have it removed, you're going to feel it pretty quickly. If you make a bad financial choice, you may not know it for many years. You have to have a good financial "physician" around to help guide you.

OPTIONS EQUAL FREEDOM

People want options. Most head off to work every day as though on a treadmill. Statistics tell us that a lot of people don't really enjoy the work they do, but they do it because they have to survive, because they have to feed the family, or because they feel caught. A lot of people do their job because that's what their mother or father did or what they were told to do in pursuit of success. That job was not necessarily something that they loved. But whether or not people love their job, as they're earning money, they want to know that somewhere along the way, they have options.

What do I mean by that? A good example was an executive at a nationally known pharmaceutical company who came to us many years ago. She wanted what I call a "checkup." She was about fifty-two, and she wanted to make sure she was going to be financially independent—in other words, that she'd be able to retire or do something else—by the time she was sixty.

We reviewed her cash flow needs, stock options, and financial holdings, and we were able to show her that, yes, she was going to be fine by sixty. Then I said to her, "How would you like to be financially independent by fifty-five? Instead of sixty, how would you like to know that when you walked into the office after your fifty-fifth birthday, being there was your choice?"

You could see her eyes widen. "Wow, that would be really neat." She happened to like what she did, but knowing that there was going to be a time when going to work would be wholly her choice sounded to her like a great option. We started exploring some financial choices she had; she had told us that as much as she liked the company at which she was working, she was getting phone calls from executive recruiters and other pharmaceutical companies to come and join them. Working with their offers, we showed her that if she earned a little bit more or had this much more in stock options or benefits, she could in fact accelerate her progress such that she would be financially independent at fifty-five—or sooner. Alternately, she could go back to her employer and start renegotiating her contract. Rather than just showing up, working there one day after another, one year after another, and hoping independence was going to be attained, she now was going to determine when it was.

She renegotiated her contract with her current employer, and she actually became financially independent by fifty-four. She was able to walk into her office and be there by choice, not because she had to go to work that day.

If you let people know how making better financial decisions will eventually give them more options in life, that turns them on. It can transform their lives. They can see that they can eventually do things that they want to do—to go out and contribute to society or to live in a way they'd never thought they could.

Realizing that I could have these options was a turning point for me. For the first time in my life, I saw that it was in my power to make choices that would ensure, by age fifty or sooner, that when I went into work, I would be there because I wanted to be, not because I had to be. There's a great feeling that comes with that certainty; suddenly there's no stress or anxiety, and I think that's what a lot of people want. They want to know that there are options in their life, that they can continue to work, if that's their preference, or do something else.

Making better financial choices can mean that you have those options sooner rather than later—or even that you have them at all. What keeps people from making those choices properly are what I call "the obstacles," which I'll talk about next.

CHAPTER TWO

THE OBSTACLES

The road to success is always under construction.
—Arnold Palmer

Obstacles are thoughts or ideas that people have about finance that prevent them from making better financial choices, which in turn prevents them from living life the way they wish now and achieving financial independence when they want—or, if they are already independent, from maintaining that independence and continuing to grow their wealth.

What are these obstacles? There are really two categories of obstacles: the *practical obstacles* and the *emotional obstacles*.

THE PRACTICAL OBSTACLES

There are only four practical obstacles:

- **no** specific goals in dollar terms
- **no** written document
- **no** process to achieve goals
- **no** road map

The first practical obstacle is a lack of specific goals with specific amounts of money attached to them. The most common practical obstacle people have is that while most people have an idea of how they would like to live now or in the future, they have no idea what that lifestyle will actually cost them. For example, say that you want a vacation home, an apartment in New York City, and to be able to travel someplace special once every year. Most people have goals like that, but they don't look at what those things actually cost now or in the future, including factors like what they pay in taxes or how much money they'll need to earn to pay for them. People do not define their goals and put numbers to them very well.

The second practical obstacle is that people have nothing written down in terms of a plan regarding how to achieve their goals. Since there's nothing in writing, there's really no point of reference that they can look back at a year or two years from now to see if they're on the right track or how to correct their course of action.

The third practical obstacle is that people don't have a process—a way of making decisions or taking actions that gets them there from here. They don't know how to do it. Take as an example a person who says, "I want to be vice president of the company rather than being a manager." How do they achieve it? What's required in terms of training? What's the process to moving up?

The last obstacle is that people have no road map. Again, if you're on a trip from New York to Wisconsin, you can just get on the road and know that it's up there north and west somewhere, or you can take out a road map. That map is going to make you more efficient and more effective. People have no financial road maps. With the wealth they have, no matter what it is, they have no idea if they're a quarter of the way, a third of the way, or halfway to what they need to achieve. Many times they don't even know if they have reached their goal!

These four practical obstacles can keep people from living the life they wish now and in the future, from being financially independent in the time frame they wish, and from staying financially independent.

WHAT WOULD APPLE DO?

Companies must also navigate these four practical obstacles, but how a well-run company manages them is often very different from how individuals approach them. A well-run company like Apple, for instance, has well-defined goals. Its leaders know what profit they're aiming for this year. They know the earnings per share, return on equity, and other benchmarks they have to achieve. Their goals are clear and defined in absolute numbers and percentages. I worked for a company, Merck & Co. Inc., where even though I was in the tax department, we had well-defined financial goals. We had budgets. As a department, we looked at our numbers monthly and quarterly, not just at the end of the year. A good financial plan will have well-defined goals and numbers attached to it.

The second practical obstacle is having nothing in writing. Everything in a well-run company is written; monthly and quarterly budgets are planned a year in advance, perhaps even years in advance. But typically, people don't plan in writing that far ahead with their personal finances, and that's a problem. If you don't have a well-defined goal in absolute dollar figures and/or percentages, you cannot know if you achieved your goals or make adjustments during the year if you get behind.

The third practical obstacle is having no process. A well-run company has good training. From day one, you know what your job is. You know the systems of the company, and if you don't, they offer superior training programs. Individuals do not know the steps to accomplish what they need to do; their "training" in personal finance is usually haphazard at best and is often achieved on the fly.

Finally, the fourth obstacle is having no road map. Well-run companies don't have that problem; they know where they are throughout the year. This is why companies lay people off, hire more people, or sell divisions in the middle of a year. They don't wait until the end of the year and say, "Gee, I wonder what I did last year?" They take actions during the year to make sure they meet their goals.

A good wealth advisor or financial planner will make sure that you have each of the following:

- goals in specific dollar terms
- a written document (a plan)
- processes to achieve goals
- a road map

With anything less, you have a much poorer chance of achieving what you want now and in the future. Be an Apple!

THE EMOTIONAL OBSTACLES

These are feelings and beliefs that can prevent people from living the life they wish or achieving and maintaining financial independence, even if they are progressing with the practical obstacles.

I find that the biggest emotion that stops people from doing things is fear. Fear of what? One common situation is that people have had a painful prior experience around a decision concerning money, and they're fearful of making the same mistake again. For example, we've all been in the market, and markets correct or crash, or we make a bad investment decision. If we made a bad investment decision, or the markets crashed and we lost money, we're scared to invest because we're worried that we will lose money again! This wariness could prevent some people from taking even measured risks, effectively paralyzing them.

Another fear is that of lack of knowledge. People with college degrees and career success think they should know this stuff. Sometimes they're embarrassed to be sitting with someone like me and having to admit they don't know what certain financial terms mean. To get beyond that, you have to admit to yourself that you don't know something and then go out and find the answer, rather than ignoring it or being ashamed.

Then there are the people who think that they already know everything. Did you ever meet a person you couldn't help? You couldn't make a contribution to their knowledge, because they read a book and think they're experts. That's another emotional obstacle: just thinking that you already know everything and not really admitting or understanding that actually you may not.

What are other kinds of fears? There are fears about how people might view you personally. That can be tied to your faith or simply to how you were raised. People sometimes fear that if they have great wealth, others might think they're morally corrupt and that their gains must somehow be ill gotten. There's so much good and bad around money that we get really confused with it as a society. Sometimes we feel guilty if we really have done very well in our lives compared to our families and friends, so we don't like to talk about it. That too can lead to poor financial choices.

Trust is also a big obstacle. If you've been burned by an advisor— an accountant, attorney, investment advisor, or insurance agent—you may have problems trusting someone else. Another obstacle is cost: good advice is sometimes costly, and some people don't want to pay for it, so they will hunt for something that costs less. Pundits play on these emotions. They say, "You don't have to pay anything. Just read a book. Just watch a program. You can make your own smart financial decisions." Some financial salespeople say, "Your planning is free or included in the cost to manage your investments." You have heard that "there is no thing as a free lunch." There is a cost for everything. People are so afraid of getting burned by paying a fee that they fall for these ploys—and into making ruinous choices.

A good wealth advisor or financial planner is going to be able to help you with your practical obstacles, and a good advisor also will listen to your emotional obstacles and help you to work through them. Some people may never wholly free themselves from emotional obstacles; they can, however, learn how to handle them.

How do you handle fear? If you remember the first time you had to speak before your class or a large audience, you may have been scared; but most likely, you got by it. You handled it. Maybe when you held your first child, the thought in your mind was, "What am I going to do?" But you got through it. You start handling things because that's the only way to progress. You may never lose the fear, but you learn to deal with it. It's exactly the same way with emotional obstacles. You just handle them.

DON'T LET YOUR EMOTIONAL
OBSTACLES DICTATE YOUR FUTURE

Everyone has emotional obstacles of one kind or another. Don't let them create a greater obstacle—one that prevents you from living the life you want, now and in the future. Don't let them dictate your financial choices and do you harm. Face them, and take control once and for all.

Finance is not all about figures. Helping a person live the life they want and putting together a financial plan for them is not all about numbers. I can make a person or a couple financially independent remarkably quickly. All I have to do is tell a young couple, "Don't have kids, don't buy a house; live in a shack, don't go out to movies or take vacations, eat franks and beans every day, and I'll get you there fast."

But living the life you want means being satisfied with the way in which you live now. I can get you there quickly using the advice laid out in my example above, but then you and your spouse may not be talking to each other in ten years. Life may not be satisfying to you now or in the future. Financial choices are also balanced with personal choices. This is why one of the ground rules for us is that we educate you. We'll guide and recommend, but you make all the financial decisions because financial decisions have to be made around what is important to you in life.

Let me end by telling you another story. A physician, a client of mine I've worked with for some years, came to see me one day. He was right on track for his financial plan, but he told me, "Al, I changed my mind about something. There's this property I found in Florida. I want to build my dream house there. I know it's not in my plan, and I realize that it may set me back a bit, but I want to do this, and you're going to help me to get it done."

Now, I could have said to him, "Well, Tom, it's not in your financial plan. You're not going to make your financial goals in the time frame you'd hope for. You won't have your options as quickly as you want." But honestly, I saw how passionate he was about this house, and I thought to myself, *This is important to him. This is how he wants to live his life. While he wants to have a financial plan, and he respects that, he wants this to fit into it.* So I said, "Tom, let's go to work. Let's make sure you have that."

What we did is fundamentally course correct so that house could fit into his financial plan. He's still on track, but now he has this beautiful home in Florida that he visits. He goes fishing. It's a real source of joy in his life, and that matters. That's what I mean when I say that financial planning is not all black and white and numbers—it's making sure that a plan is flexible enough to allow you to make changes so that you're living the life you want along the way.

YOU DON'T HAVE TO GIVE UP LIVING TO HAVE A LIFE

It's easy to transform a person's life if they're willing to scrape by, to eat franks and beans. It's a lot more complicated when you're dealing with the vast majority of people. They have their wants and needs, and they have things in their lives that go wrong: they have a problem with a child, an illness comes up, they lose their job, or their marriage ends. These rough patches are all part of the normal course of life. But with a solid plan, you can deal with the chasms, bumps, and potholes that come up along the way. Making that happen is what's important in my work with people. It's how we continually transform lives.

One of my long-term clients is also a good friend—Bob, a physician who I met in the early nineties. At that time, medicine was going through a lot of changes, and many popular pundits were out on the circuit telling young doctors to pay off their debts and hunker down because things were not going to be the same and physicians would be hitting hard times. They were really spreading panic. Bob was just starting out in his specialty practice when he came in. We really connected, although my advice to him was the total opposite of anything he had heard from others. I was telling him to keep his debt and to look to his cash flow. He asked me, "Why is everyone out there telling me something different?"

I explained that the pundits give advice that sounds easy and simple to people. Pundits patronize people and aren't telling them what real finance is. I said, "You do it my way, and you'll get wherever you want in life." Over the next twenty years, he not only created a successful practice but also other businesses. He makes tremendous amounts of money and is very wealthy today, but he's still that down-to-earth guy. More importantly, he lives life the way he wants.

When I remarried some years ago, I asked Bob and his wife to my wedding. The chief operating officer (COO) of my company, Traust Sollus Wealth Management, happened to be sitting with them at the reception. Bob turned around to the COO and said, "You know, Al Zdenek is the best thing that ever happened to me." My COO was kind of stunned, especially since Bob's wife was right next to him and was listening to the conversation. Half-jokingly, he said, "I'm sure you meant except for Sally, right?"

Without even a beat, Bob said, "No, I mean her too."

She didn't argue!

CHAPTER THREE

BECOMING THE MASTER
OF YOUR CASH FLOW

Number one, cash is king.
—Jack Welch

A t Traust Sollus, our philosophy is that we don't believe that penny-pinching—skipping Starbucks to have a cheap latte or giving up whatever it is that makes you happy—is the way to live your life and take on the challenge of creating and achieving a financial plan. Our philosophy is that if you make better financial decisions around your cash flow, then you'll waste less money on avoidable expenses and will give less money to the government. That will empower you to have that money for your lifestyle now, to save and/or build your wealth for how you want to live in retirement, and to achieve financial independence. We call this finding more cash flow the Integrated Cash Flow Management Approach℠. Our methodology of personal financial planning is the Wealth Building Formula®. This chapter will be focused on these, which are designed to make you become master of your cash flow, achieve the way you wish to live now, and achieve or maintain financial independence.

THE TWO KINDS OF PERSONAL FINANCIAL PLANNERS

There are two types of personal financial planners. One is called a goals-based planner. If you go to a goals-based planner, you will be asked what kind of goals you have in life. You might say, "I want to be retired by sixty," "I want a vacation home in Colorado," "I want my children to be educated," or "I want a larger home." The goals-based planner will help you calculate the numbers for the different "pots of money" you need for those goals. Then the conversation becomes about how to save for them and how to invest and make your money grow.

We are cash-flow planners, which is the second type. Cash-flow planners are much less common than goals-based planners. A cash-flow planner will ask the same questions concerning goals as a goals-based planner because it is important to know your goals. But there's one big difference: We just don't say, "What do you want?", take the goals you give us, and concentrate on those areas. Rather, we look at every aspect of your financial life. We are out to find more free cash flow. Free cash flow is cash left after all bills have been paid. To find the most free cash flow you can; you must look at every part of your financial life.

If we find more free cash flow working with you (and there has never been a case in which we have not), you can spend this excess cash flow on your lifestyle. Or, if you save and invest it, you could:

- achieve your financial goals more quickly;
- have more wealth at the end of the time frame of your plan; or
- reduce the risk in your investment portfolio.

We will discuss all of the above and what they mean as we progress through this book. But let's concentrate on finding more free cash flow to invest or what we call "investable cash."

For example, if you had the goals I listed above but neglected to mention debt, insurance, where you work, or how you work, we would explore those areas with you. If you have a business, we'd want to know how the business is running, how you are pricing your product or service, and what profit you are earning. If you have a job, we'd ask how you're negotiating your contract or compensation. How are you choosing your benefits and determining the contributions and investment selections of your 401(k)? We look at all these aspects of your financial life because by doing that, we can find more investable cash.

Financial choices don't have just one effect on your finances; any one decision can affect many areas of your financial life. These decisions can use more of your cash flow or provide more investable cash. It is your choice.

For example, if you're buying a house, probably the first thing you'll ask yourself is, "Can I afford the mortgage?" But buying a house is just not a cash flow decision or a debt decision. It's also an investment decision, an insurance decision, an estate decision, and a tax decision. There are many financial areas that your purchase of a house is going to affect, and if you're not looking at all of those areas, you may not make the best financial choice—the choice that will help you to keep building wealth, to get to your goals in life, and to live the life you wish now.

I've touched on this analogy before, but properly executed, the Integrated Cash Flow Management Approach℠ comes down to running your finances as a well-run company does. When you think of well-run company like Apple, they have the same issues that we all have. When they make a financial decision, it affects many, many areas.

I worked at Merck & Co. Inc. in their corporate tax department. Merck wanted to build a plant in another state, which is somewhat like buying a house. But that is where the similarity ends. As a well-run company, they considered all of the areas of financial impact, unlike most home buyers. As I said before, it's not only a decision as to whether you can afford the house itself (cash flow) but also the other issues it affects: it's an investment decision, an insurance decision, a tax decision, a debt decision, and an estate decision. Companies don't call it an "estate" decision; to them, it's a "shareholder wealth" decision. They take this all into account to make the best financial choice. The Integrated Cash Flow Management Approach℠ comes down to making decisions with the same mind-set that well-run businesses apply to their financial situations, applying the best practices toward managing their cash flow, finding more investable cash, and growing more wealth.

WE WORK WITH SMART PEOPLE . . . AND MAKE THEM SMARTER

At Traust Sollus, we meet many highly successful individuals—executives, entrepreneurs, business owners, physicians, and professionals—and these people are very bright. Most are in their midforties to midfifties; have become masters of their businesses, careers, and professions; and are often among the very best at what they do. But what they normally have not mastered is their cash flow. As I have said before, time and time again, clients who are very successful in life come to meet with us and say, "I visit my accountant at the end of the year to do my tax return. They tell me how much I've earned and how much I owe, and I think to myself, *I made all that money? What did I do with it?*"

When first coming to us, clients don't know how to control and become masters of their cash flow. But through our Integrated Cash Flow Management Approach℠, we make them masters of their money. We give them control of their cash flow so that they can preserve their wealth or build additional wealth to do the things in life they want, now or in the future.

A good example is a client I had, Chuck, who was a very senior executive of a Fortune 200 company. He was about sixty years old and had done very well, so he figured he could retire and notified his company that in six months, he was going to leave. He had a couple of beautiful homes, and in preparation for retirement, he took money out of savings and paid off the mortgages on both of them. But then he wisely decided he'd better come and talk to me for a financial checkup.

After putting him through a rigorous financial review, I said, "Chuck, I have some good news and bad news for you. The bad news is that you don't have enough assets to generate the cash flow you need to live the way you want now and for the rest of your life." He looked at me, shocked.

"The good news is, you know those mortgages that you paid off? Just take them out again. If you take them out again, you'll be able to generate that needed cash flow from your investments, you'll have more tax sheltering from the interest deduction giving you even more free cash flow, and you'll be able to live the way you wish now and in the future."

Chuck had made a poor financial choice and didn't know it. And if he hadn't come in for the checkup, he would have retired at sixty, and he and his wife might have lived for many years feeling okay. But somewhere in his seventies, or maybe a little later, slowly their cash flow may have gotten tight. They would have had to cut back on their spending, and they would have never have known why. Having that checkup saved them from that.

Making better financial choices and also understanding what it means for your big picture is extremely important. That's what the Integrated Cash Flow Management Approach℠ is all about: making you a master of your money.

We're not out to make you CPAs, attorneys, insurance agents, or other experts like that. We're out to make sure that you know where your money is going and where you are right now, that you have the wealth you need at any time in the future, and that you know how to manage and build that wealth. Knowledge is power—and who better to have power over your future than you?

DEBT ISN'T ALWAYS THE ENEMY

Keep in mind that there's nothing wrong with paying off debt. It's wrong, though, if you're paying it off without considering how that affects your current wealth and cash flow generation now and in the future. I think people would probably agree that Warren Buffett is a pretty savvy business investor—and Warren Buffett's companies have debt. Well-run companies have debt. They have debt for a reason; by balancing debt with what is held in assets, more wealth might be generated. I'm not encouraging you to go out and incur debt just to have it, much less to run up credit card debt for frivolous consumption. But exploring the opportunities of having debt may allow you to balance more wealth generation and is a savvy thing to consider. We'll talk more extensively about using debt smarter in a later chapter.

We do see a couple of different kinds of clients whose cash flow management problems get them into difficulties. The first group is those who've come out of years of education—physicians, professionals, or young executives, for instance—and who suddenly start making real money. They're feeling good and are inclined to treat themselves to some rewards: a big house, new car, and travel. They run up some big bills, and then all of a sudden, they find out that cash is tight. Normally, when you sit down with those people and make them aware of how it has happened, it's pretty easy to correct.

But other, more ingrained habits—like spending more than you should over a career's worth of time—aren't so easy to break. We gradually get acclimated to this way of living; we get used to keeping up with the Joneses, or there are things that we want and think we should have. We're hoping that the next bonus or raise from our job or our business is going to make everything okay, but it never quite catches up.

Another type of person is what I'll call a "person of circumstances"—and those circumstances are sometimes not good. They've lived for fifteen or twenty years with excess cash flow. They've lived within a certain budget. They've even saved some money on the side. But then something happens: they lose their jobs, or their business falters. They have a tough time finding a job. Eventually they do find one, but they've had this interruption in cash flow, and if they didn't have adequate savings put aside, that interruption can really damage what they have built up. They still have the groceries to pay for, the house to support, the kids to educate and the mortgage to pay. The tragedy is when you have a person who's been an executive or business owner who has lived a nice lifestyle but hasn't saved enough because they didn't know how much they had to save or assumed that their business or company pension would cover their retirement. Suddenly, in their mid to late fifties, they're thrown out of work or suffer a bad patch, and all of a sudden their retirement plans evaporate.

This is not uncommon; in fact, we've seen this every time there's been a crash in the market, whether it's been the 1987 crash; the crash and corrections of 2000, 2001, and 2002; or the most recent crash of 2008. In each of these, we've met with people who'd had a time frame in which they had wanted to retire, and all of a sudden their 401(k)s became "201(k)s"—they got cut in half. They found out that they didn't have the wealth they'd need, which meant they had to work longer or else have less cash flow in their retirement years.

Bill was a client I had in 1987 who was in the real estate business. He was a high-level executive in a big firm that built shopping malls and bought and sold very large properties. He and his wife, Mary, enjoyed a nice lifestyle. They'd invested in some of these shopping centers and industrial parks because the company always kept shares for executive retirement. What they didn't realize is that they had all their eggs in one basket. All of a sudden the 1987 recession hit, and what suffered the most at that time was real estate. A lot of people ended up giving their real estate back to the banks and declaring bankruptcy. Bill was sixty-one; Mary was a little younger. All of these properties that had made them wealthy on paper were suddenly worth a whole lot less. What was worse was that his company had to downsize, so they asked him to leave. Now he had no income and an almost-worthless portfolio.

WORKING THE NUMBERS

By focusing on their current wealth for the first time, Bill and Mary understood what kind of wealth they actually needed to live the lifestyle they wished. We began to go through the holdings in their portfolio and to decide what they could sell, as well as what they couldn't or shouldn't. Some properties they had to sell at a sacrifice, but it was essential to diversify so that they could have cash flow to get back to the life they wanted to live now and also be able to retire down the line.

At that time, Bill didn't think he was going to be able to retire until his mid seventies. But through our Integrated Cash Flow Management Approach℠ and by creating their Wealth Building Formula® (which we'll get into in a later chapter), within three or four years we were able to make up a good deal of the assets they'd had before, and we restored their cash flow. He and his wife have been enjoying the good life in retirement now for over twenty years.

Again, here were intelligent people who'd made some poor financial choices that came close to ruining them, largely because they were poorly educated about finances and managing cash flow. Poor financial choices can come back to haunt you, even if you're doing well.

IT'S ALL ABOUT YOUR CHOICES

When physicians first get out of medical school, they are often offered jobs with medical practices, networks, or education. They have choices to make; one employer might offer $350,000 a year; another might offer $325,000; and a third might offer to pay them $400,000 a year. If they don't understand finance and can't adequately judge the benefits and other opportunities each of these groups is offering in addition to salary, they can make the wrong financial decision.

The group that offers $400,000 may not have a pension plan or other benefits like helping to pay off school loans, for instance. That means you have to fund those items for yourself, which might effectively cut the cash flow you're making down to $320,000, whereas the group that offered you what looked like less might actually be offering you more once you factor in those extras.

It's the same way with a business. When people start businesses, they normally go through what I call the "breakeven process." They say to themselves, "I have overhead like rent, salaries to pay people, utilities, and other costs," and they can list these exactly. Their thinking is, "If I bring in enough sales to cover expenses, I've broken even," and they think they're succeeding.

This is not realistic. Success doesn't mean that you just pay for your overhead; it means that you're also making the money that's going to allow you to live the lifestyle you wish, pay your taxes, and be able to save for retirement or be financially independent in the time frame you choose. That's why, when you're making your budget for a business, you should add what you have to earn as a salary, what you have to pay in taxes, and what to put aside annually for your financial independence. Most business owners don't do that, so they have a business that goes on for years and years and may grow very large, but they haven't amassed the savings that they should have to ensure that they're going to accomplish what they want. Granted, their business may be worth something someday. But it's a big danger to bet your future on what your business might be worth someday. You could hit a rough patch in the economy or face stiff competition. You or other key people could fall ill, which could hurt the value of the business and ruin your plans for an early exit or when you're close to retirement.

The bottom line is that the vast majority of people don't have enough financial education or financial background to make informed choices about their finances, nor do they take sufficient time to sit down and really look at, "What kind of cash flow will I have coming in? And what do I have to do with it?"

THE FUNNELS

The analogy I use to describe how most people think about their cash flow is the "Three Funnel System," or simply "The Funnels." Most people think of the cash flowing into their lives like it's coming to them through a funnel: their paycheck. Withholding taxes for the government come out of that check in the funnel, as well as unemployment taxes and all the other taxes the government imposes, so already you see a lot less money than your salary once it's gone through this funnel.

What's left then flows into another funnel, which is the "Things We Have to Pay" funnel. That would include your mortgage, personal loans, car loans, and credit cards. This funnel is your debt.

The money that flows from the debt funnel flows into the last funnel, which is what we'd call "lifestyle"—it covers all other expenses like food, utilities, vacations—expenses that are part of life. Whatever is left after this last funnel—if there's anything—is what people see as money they can then save for their future.

THE CASH FLOW FUNNELS

HOW PEOPLE NORMALLY THINK OF CASH FLOW AND SAVING

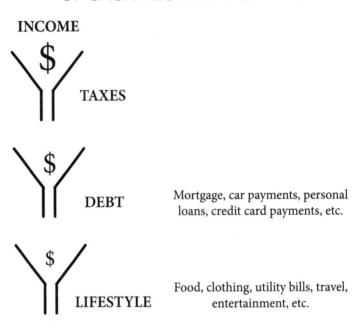

INCOME

$

TAXES

$

DEBT — Mortgage, car payments, personal loans, credit card payments, etc.

$

LIFESTYLE — Food, clothing, utility bills, travel, entertainment, etc.

$ FREE CASH FLOW

Now you can finally save!

But a well-run business sees cash flow very differently. A well-run business has the same three funnels. Money flows into the first funnel in the form of sales, and like us, businesses have to pay taxes out of that. The second funnel is where they pay debt. The last funnel, the one individuals think of as "lifestyle" is what a company calls "operations." They have to pay for the heat, lights, employee salaries, benefits, and other costs. What is left is profit, or earnings per share.

Stockholders like to see share values rise, and if earnings per share go up year after year, that means the stock price also tends to go up. If earnings per share is flat, that could mean the stock price is flat. If earnings per share go down, then your stock price most likely will go down.

What happens to the executive team at those companies whose stock goes down every year? They get fired. So they have a vested interest in making sure that after the money goes through those three funnels, the money at the end is a higher amount than it was last year so that the earnings per share is higher than it was last year.

How do executives do that? When the money is coming into the first funnel, they're starting to make choices like, "Do I open up that factory, hire this person, fire that person?" They want to make sure the bottom line will be higher than it was last year. They are focused on a goal, and their choices are aligned with that goal.

People don't run their cash flow like well-run businesses. Money comes in, it goes out, and they hope that there's something left at the end of the year. Companies don't think like that. They target the bottom line or profit. So what you want to do is to target your money like a well-run business does. You want to say, "If I have a certain amount of wealth now, and I want it to be more, this much has to be left over after my expenses. If it isn't, then either my expenses have to change, or the way I make money has to change." That's the way to run your cash flow like a well-run business does.

If you find that you're stressed and anxious about your cash flow, and there doesn't seem to be much (if any) extra at the end of the year, then even if you have a good amount of wealth, you could see your wealth stagnate or go down, leaving you without the cash flow you need. But you have a choice. You can go year after year, hoping that your goal will be achieved by the end of the year, or you can start to target the amounts that you need and make sure that you make choices aligned with a sound financial plan to hit the target.

KNOW WHAT YOU ARE SPENDING

If you don't know, how can you plan your wealth and your future cash flow for you and your loved ones? It's like deciding to just get in your car and drive without knowing how much fuel you have. This does not mean you necessarily have to spend less; just know what you are spending.

How do you accomplish this? When most people first come in to see us, they have no idea what their spending is. We ask them to put together the numbers on what they spent for that month or over a three-month or a six-month period. They need to get out those bank statements and follow the cash flow. As CPAs, we can also calculate approximate overall spending for you, but it is important that you know where your spending is. Is what you have coming in adequate to cover your expenses, or are you borrowing to make ends meet? That's the first step; knowledge is power.

When we enter into this process with clients, we can see how much they earned for the year and how much they paid in taxes. If they had to borrow money at the end of the year or during the year, and they had it take away from their savings, we know that they're not actually meeting their cash flow needs. If we see that they have a surplus, then we can see if it's enough for them to live the lifestyle they wish, now and in the future. This also allows us to see if there is wasteful spending and opportunities for finding investable cash. In any case, just as in a well-run company, it's critical to really know your numbers. It is also very important to check this annually: revisit how much money you actually need for the lifestyle you're living, and see what's left. Companies that do not know how much they are spending are in big trouble.

People often underestimate; we had a couple who judged that their household spending was $600,000 per year. But when we looked at what they earned and what they paid in taxes, we found that they could not account for some $200,000. Once that cash flow spending is accurately determined, we can see more clearly what is needed, where the problems are, and even more important, where the opportunities lie.

People lead busy lives and don't pay attention to where their money is going. Sometimes it's going places they aren't even aware of. When it's pointed out to them, they often realize, "I don't really need that," or, "I'm overpaying for this," and we can find them more cash flow.

One example is home insurance, especially for someone who owns more than one or two homes. We've had clients who, unbeknownst to them, were paying $30,000 for their home insurance. They didn't realize that when they'd made a claim two or three years ago, the insurance company didn't like it and had jacked up their rates. Too often these kinds of bills are put on autopay and never reviewed. With those clients, we were able to reduce their home insurance bills from $30,000 to $8,000 a year, with better protection! This is not unusual.

ARE YOU MAXIMIZING YOUR BENEFITS?

Another example of a common problem was an executive who, because he didn't understand the benefits his company was offering, like pension or savings plan choices, wasn't actually fully participating in them, even though he thought that he was. He came to see us when he was in his late fifties and had been working with his company for a long time. We pointed out to him that there was a particular deferred compensation plan that would allow him to put away his total bonuses for the year. This strategy would save him over $200,000 a year in taxes. He didn't need all the pay he made, and this way, he could add another $200,000 or more per year to his savings without even feeling it—a nice investable cash find.

Another recent example was a couple who overpaid their taxes by almost $125,000. The CPA preparing their tax returns did not realize the error. It was not until we reviewed their income taxes that we told them to have their CPA contact the government and get the cash back.

People get busy and don't focus on where they're spending money or who's sending them the bills except when it's outlandish or their cash is tight. That's why we're always able to find money for people for investable cash that they don't even know they have. In fact, in thirty years in business, having spoken to literally hundreds of people, we have never—not once—been unable to find, at minimum, tens of thousands of dollars a year, and sometimes hundreds of thousands of dollars a year, in excess cash flow. In some cases, millions of dollars are found through better tax planning, reviewing benefits, looking at how a business owner is running his or her company, or scrutinizing expenses.

CHAPTER FOUR

THE WEALTH BUILDING FORMULA®

*Your economic security does not lie in your job; it lies in your own
power to produce—to think, to learn, to create, to adapt.
That's true financial independence.*
—Stephen R. Covey

At Traust Sollus, our philosophy is that people should live the lifestyle they wish now; if they focus on their cash flow and don't waste money on imprudent expenses or pay excess taxes and make better financial choices, this should be possible. I've explained our Integrated Cash Flow Management Approach℠ and how to look at your financial choices as a well-run business would. The next financial detail to ascertain is how much wealth do I need now or as "core" wealth—wealth that will keep you financially independent. Our methodology for doing this: the Wealth Building Formula®.

You'll recall the three funnels I talked about in the previous chapter and that well-run businesses look at cash flow by targeting their spending because they have to make sure the bottom line is going to be higher than it was last year. Individuals, on the other hand, just hope the extra money's there; too often, they're not aware whether it is or isn't.

The Wealth Building Formula® provides an individual with benchmarks on what wealth is needed and the way to make the 100 percent correct financial decision to grow and retain that wealth. Let's deal with benchmarks first. Benchmarks are what well-run companies have that individuals don't; Apple and other successful companies all have financial benchmarks or key performance indicators that allow them to assess things like, "Are we doing better than our peers or worse than our peers? Are we hitting our targets?" Among their benchmarks might be earnings per share, return on equity, or other measures. As individuals, we don't think in terms of earnings per share. Most people don't even know how much they need to save. They don't have a long-term investment return objective or rate of return needed from their investment portfolios to make it all work. They just hope it's there. For example, with investments, they just look to see, "Did I do better than the S&P 500 this quarter?" That's not the same thing as creating your target. But you can't have a target without a plan that provides you with benchmarks and a way to make the right financial decisions.

The Wealth Building Formula® allows people to put their goals into exact numbers. It creates a clear process by which they can make good decisions—one that allows them to see where they are on their road map. Are they financially independent today? What about in five years? Are they on the right track?

The Wealth Building Formula® looks at what cash flow you need today to live the life you wish. As an example, let's assume you needed $750,000 a year to live—to pay your taxes, to cover expenses, and to save toward building your wealth. You're bringing in this income either through working for someone or via your business. But someday, you want to have the option to leave your job or sell that business, either to do something else or to retire. If you can get that same $750,000 you require every year from your investments, adjusted for inflation (you can count on inflation rising each year), then you're financially independent. You can do whatever you want. You don't have to go to work. That's the cash flow you need.

The Wealth Building Formula® is a straightforward equation:

$$C \times T \times \% \text{ RETURN} = \$\$\$$$

C is investable cash or the amount of wealth you need to generate cash flow. *T* is the time frame in which you want to gain your financial independence. *% Return* is the long-term investment return objective that you need (from your investment portfolio or from finding more investable cash) to make sure this all works and that the cash flow you are generating equals the cash flow that you'll need in today's dollars at the point when you retire or decide to do something else. When we work with clients, we use this equation to make sure that each of them has their own personalized Wealth Building Formula® and their own benchmarks to track.

What kind of cash flow do you need to make sure that you can live the lifestyle you wish? What does that equate to in wealth? What types of investments do you need so your amount of wealth generates the needed cash flow? What kind of time frame are we talking about to get to that point? Then, what percentage return do you need? What long-term investment return objective should you have so that you can properly construct your portfolio and balance it with the risk you wish to take (which we will talk about in another chapter)?

EVERYONE IS DIFFERENT

Knowing your personal Wealth Building Formula® is critical to achieving the financial independence you want, within a time frame that's workable for your goals and how you wish to live now. Once you've nailed that down, then the second and just as important part is *working* your formula. How do you work it? When you're making financial decisions, your Wealth Building Formula® is the yardstick against which you measure them.

The numbers represented in the equation $C \times T \times \% \ Return = \$\$\$$ are variables. A change in one of the variables on the left side of the equation will have an effect on the right side—the cash flow for which you are planning. A change on the right side of the equation will have an effect on one or all of the variables on the left side. Knowing what these variables are, the effects caused by changes in any one of them, and targeting and keeping track of them just as a well-run business does will allow you to make the right financial choices.

Let's look at an example: If you can save more than you target annually to C (your wealth), then the T (time) to get there will be reduced; you can earn less *% Return*; or the *$$$* (cash flow) you are targeting could be more.

WEALTH BUILDING FORMULA®

C x T x % Return = $$$

Investable Cash x Time x % Return = Annual Cash Flow for
Financial Independence

How Does It Work?

If you have to save <u>$100,000</u> per year ("C") but you actually save
<u>$125,000</u> (or more than you have to), the following can happen:

↑C x ↓T x ↓% Return = ↑$$$

T can <u>decrease,</u> *% Return* can <u>decrease,</u> or
you have <u>more</u> cash flow due to <u>increased</u> wealth

If you have to save <u>$100,000</u> per year ("C") but actually you save
only <u>$75,000</u> (or less than you have to),
the following can happen:

↓C x ↑T x ↑% Return = ↓$$$

T can <u>increase,</u> *% Return* can <u>increase,</u> or
you have <u>less</u> cash flow due to <u>decreased</u> wealth

If you save less than your annual target to *C* or use money from your
wealth for some purpose, then *T* will be increased; you will have to
raise the *% Return* to achieve your *$$$*, or your *$$$* will be less.

Any financial choice increases or decreases C. Knowing this will allow you to make choices knowing that you are increasing or decreasing T or *% Return* in your portfolio. Or, if you choose to keep T and *% Return* the same, you will affect *$$$*—your targeted cash flow.

Let's say that you need to save $100,000 per year to achieve your *$$$* (cash flow) goals in X number of years. This year, you find a way to save $125,000—more than your target for C. By adding more than what was required to your wealth, you could decrease your T (time) to independence, or you could reduce your *% Return* needed from your investments to keep the same cash flow (*$$$*).

Conversely, say that you had to save $100,000 per year to make your goal but could only save $75,000. By not adding enough to your C, you may have to increase T (delaying your independence), increase the *% Return* (thus increasing risk), or reduce the *$$$*. Got it?

Here's another view of how the formula works: A financial choice comes along—you want to put a $500,000 addition or improvement on your home. You could go out and borrow the money, or you could take the money from the C (wealth) you have.

If you borrow it, you're going to pay it back over a period of time. You will not have to decrease C (wealth), so you do not have to increase T (time) or *% Return*. Borrowing the money does not decrease C, and thus your formula is unaffected. But if you take the improvement funds from your C, then you will have to increase T or *% Return* for it not to affect your *$$$* (targeted cash flow). By the way, this is what we mean by "working" your Wealth Building Formula®. I am assuming in this example that you will be able to absorb the annual payments of debt from your current cash flow without affecting your savings target each year.

As another example, say that you have a $500,000 mortgage on your house that costs you about $25,000 a year. You're one of those people who decides, "You know what? I'm going to pay it off quicker. I have a good job. I have the extra cash flow for it. So I'm not only going to pay my $25,000, I'm going to pay an extra $25,000 each year." Again, deciding to accelerate their mortgage payments is a very common choice people make. But suppose that instead of putting that $25,000 into the house, you added it to your C. This might get you to your financial goals quicker, or you might have more cash flow ($$$) when you get to the end of your T and reach retirement or independence. People accelerate payments all of the time and don't realize that they are just adding more time in which they "have" to work, are increasing the risk in their portfolios, or are setting themselves up to have less cash flow when they retire.

KNOWLEDGE IS POWER—AND IT GIVES YOU OPTIONS

I had a physician client who was just getting out of his residency program and had significant debt. He wanted to pay off his student loans over five years. By working his Wealth Building Formula®, I was able to show him that if he did that, he wasn't going to be able to save sufficient money out of his cash flow to support his long-term financial plan. However, he had the option to pay off the loans over twenty-five years, which meant the yearly payments were a lot less, and thus he'd have more money to save now. If he chose that option and added it to his C, his time frame became shorter because his cash flow became a lot higher, and he didn't have to get as high a *% Return* on his portfolio, which meant he could invest his money at less risk.

This same physician also had two car loans that he was trying to pay off as quickly as possible. I showed him that he could save

$10,000 of additional investable cash per year by paying these car loans off slower so that his payments weren't as high, and he could add the excess cash flow to his *C*, which got him to his goals faster. He's been a client for twenty-five years and is now enjoying financial independence. I recently got an e-mail from him, thanking me for transforming his attitude toward money and his life all those years ago.

There's a lot of conflicting advice on personal finance, but it's important to remember that most of these pundits and "experts" are speaking generally to the masses. The fact is, the same financial choices will not be suitable for everyone. By having a customized Wealth Building Formula® tailored to your needs and goals—by understanding your formula and working it properly—you can make the right financial choice for you or at least see what the result of your choice will be. I've never had two clients whose formulas were exactly the same. No client lives exactly the way another does. Your formula has to be customized to the way you wish to live, now and in your future. There are some people who, if I said to them, "Don't pay off your mortgage quickly," and showed them how this could get them to their planning goals two or three years faster, might feel comfortable doing so. Some may not and would instead choose to work longer. It is up to you!

There could be another client who tells me, "You know, Al, I can see it would benefit us, but we can't sleep at night with this debt. We have to pay it off." Well, if you can't sleep at night and it's going to cause you stress and anxiety, then pay off that debt quicker; just understand, it means that you're going to work longer and harder in life or take on more risk in your investment portfolio for the cash flow you need. The important lesson here is that you need to know what the effect of a choice is so you can make an *informed* choice.

I equate the Wealth Building Formula® to having a physical exam. Suppose you wake up one day with a pain in your chest. You have this pain for days, maybe even for weeks. You try to ignore it, but you can't. What do you do? By this time, you're scared to go to the doctor because he or she might tell you that it's serious. Ultimately you do go, and the doctor either tells you that it is in fact serious or that it's not. At least knowing what the problem is means that you can make an informed decision about how to proceed. But if you live with the stress and anxiety of the unknown and don't do anything about it, then you don't put yourself in control of the situation. That's what the Wealth Building Formula® does: it allows you to make a series of informed choices to get you to your goal, and it takes away the stress and anxiety of not knowing where you stand.

IT CHANGED MY LIFE

I am an example of this; I saw the power of what having something like the Wealth Building Formula® can do for you because of what it did for me. When I started looking at my plan many years ago, my goal was to be independent by the time I was fifty. I made it by forty-eight. It was solely due to the Wealth Building Formula® and making informed and better financial choices.

What are some valuable ways for a person to work their Wealth Building Formula®? Let's say you are a business owner. Someone makes you a purchase offer for $10 million, and you're eager to accept it. But if you haven't calculated your Wealth Building Formula® or don't know what your current cash flow needs are or what kind of wealth you need to have to create that cash flow now and in the future, then you don't know whether or not to make that deal.

If your advisor told you that you'd need to get $12 million for your business to have the cash flow you require now and for the rest of your life, you could then go back to the potential buyer with that number. In the event that they won't go any higher, you can take that offer and also understand what you need to do with the money in order to make up the shortfall between what you have now and what you'll need in the future. Alternately, you can take steps to increase the value of your business. Do you raise your prices, cut expenses, hire more people, build a new location, or buy a second business to merge with the first? Knowing the effect these choices will have on your cash flow provides another valuable lesson in working your Wealth Building Formula®.

Working your formula means you're doing things with a purpose that's aligned with your plan, not flying blind on a wing and a prayer, hoping that you've made the right financial choice. Starting sooner, as opposed to later, is another critical factor, as we'll discuss in the next chapter on the power of compounding.

CHAPTER FIVE

THE POWER
OF COMPOUNDING

Compound interest is the greatest mathematical
discovery of all time.
—Albert Einstein

Do you want to make the best-informed financial decision all of the time? First, create your Wealth Building Formula®. Then, understand the principal of compounding. If you understand and use the principal of compounding along with what we call the Tax Saving Savings Effect (explained in the next chapter), you will always make the 100 percent correct financial choice.

Human beings are linear thinkers. Humans don't think in terms of complicated formulas; that's why we need calculators, like calculating mortgages. For example, if we're taking a trip from New York to Wisconsin, we tend to think in terms of straight lines; we don't consider all the twists and turns between here and there.

Money growth doesn't work in a linear fashion either; it can compound in a geometric way. Banks in the nineteenth century used simple interest calculations, but they very rapidly realized that compounding was a far better way to make money. Albert Einstein was also purported to have said, "Those who understand compound interest make it, those who don't pay it."

Most people don't really understand the power of compounding, and the lack of that knowledge can hinder their ability to make better financial choices. People intellectually comprehend compounding on some level but usually not with any real clarity—or they simply don't believe it. One good analogy is to think of how bacteria grow in Petri dishes. A bacterial colony starts out slowly; one cell becomes two, which become four, and so on. But at a certain point the doubling really takes off, and you're talking about much larger numbers being created in the same span of time. This is sort of how compounding works: It starts slow. It takes time. But if you're steady with it, it gets to a point where it grows at a much more rapid pace.

With that in mind, let's explore the power of compounding and the "saving now versus later" concept. Let's use two people as examples: the Go-Getter and the Slowpoke in the illustration. Compounding always rewards the person who saves sooner. Our Go-Getter has an extra $5,500 coming in annually, and she starts to save it. After ten years, she stops saving and just lets it grow and compound. Meanwhile, the Slowpoke also has that extra $5,500 coming in, but she finds ways to spend it. She goes along like that for ten years, then starts saving in the eleventh year.

THE POWER OF COMPOUNDING
Savings now versus later

	The Go-Getter!		The Slowpoke	
Year	Contribution	Wealth	Contribution	Wealth
1	$5,500	$5,885	$0	$0
2	$5,500	12,182	0	0
3	$5,500	18,920	0	0
4	$5,500	26,129	0	0
5	$5,500	33,843	0	0
6	$5,500	42,097	0	0
7	$5,500	50,929	0	0
8	$5,500	60,379	0	0
9	$5,500	70,490	0	0
10	$5,500	81,310	0	0
11	$0	87,001	5,500	5,885
12	$0	93,092	5,500	12,182
13	$0	99,608	5,500	18,920
14	$0	106,581	5,500	26,129
15	$0	114,041	5,500	33,843
16	$0	122,024	5,500	42,097
17	$0	130,566	5,500	50,929
18	$0	139,705	5,500	60,379
19	$0	149,485	5,500	70,490
20	$0	159,949	5,500	81,310
21	$0	171,145	5,500	92,886
22	$0	183,125	5,500	105,274
23	$0	195,944	5,500	118,528
24	$0	209,660	5,500	132,710
25	$0	224,336	5,500	147,884
26	$0	240,040	5,500	164,121
27	$0	256,843	5,500	181,495
28	$0	274,822	5,500	200,084
29	$0	294,059	5,500	219,975
30	$0	314,643	5,500	241,258
31	$0	336,668	5,500	264,032
32	$0	360,235	5,500	288,399
33	$0	385,452	5,500	314,472
34	$0	412,433	5,500	342,370
35	$0	441,303	5,500	372,221
36	$0	472,195	5,500	404,161
37	$0	505,248	5,500	438,337
38	$0	540,616	5,500	474,906
39	$0	578,459	5,500	514,034
40	$0	618,951	5,500	555,902
41	$0	662,277	5,500	600,700
42	$0	708,637	5,500	648,634
43	$0	**$758,241**	5,500	**$699,923**
Total Contributions	**$55,000**		**$181,500**	

7% assumed rate of return

By year forty-three, our Go-Getter (who put away $55,000 for those first ten years and then didn't save any more) has more money than the Slowpoke (who waited until year eleven and then saved for thirty-three years)—$181,500. The Slowpoke saved more than three times the amount of the Go-Getter but was still behind!

The lesson is clear: it takes you longer to create wealth if you don't take advantage of compounding. If you save later, you have to save longer and work harder to end up with less than the person who saves and takes advantage of compounding sooner.

When I show clients the chart I've included here, they'll often look at it, shrug, and say, "Al, I'm fifty years old. I may not have forty-three years!"

I say, "Yes, that may be true. But you know what? You're not starting from zero like the illustration. You've already accumulated wealth, and the choices you make over the next ten, twenty, or thirty years are going to decide how much more money and how much more wealth you have in the future versus now. You can be the Slowpoke and have less, or you can be the Go-Getter and have more." The rules apply no matter where you are in your life.

For the clients I work with, $5,500 a year is an extremely modest amount, so suppose that instead of that smaller amount, you put away $100,000 per year. Then suppose that you're the person who continues to save beyond the tenth year. The Slowpoke never catches up with you, and the gap of wealth between the both of you is just tremendous. See the illustration!

The key lesson to harnessing the power of compounding is to save now rather than later. If you're looking at our Integrated Cash Flow Management Approach℠, that means when you find more investable cash, save it now rather than later.

THE POWER OF COMPOUNDING
Savings now versus later

	The Go-Getter!			The Slowpoke	
	Savings $100,000/yr from year #1			Savings $100,000/yr from year #11	
Year	Contribution	Wealth		Contribution	Wealth
1	$100,000	$107,000		$0	$0
2	$100,000	221,490		0	0
3	$100,000	343,994		0	0
4	$100,000	475,074		0	0
5	$100,000	615,329		0	0
6	$100,000	765,402		0	0
7	$100,000	925,980		0	0
8	$100,000	1,097,799		0	0
9	$100,000	1,281,645		0	0
10	$100,000	1,478,360		0	0
11	$100,000	1,688,845		100,000	107,000
12	$100,000	1,914,064		100,000	221,490
13	$100,000	2,155,049		100,000	343,994
14	$100,000	2,412,902		100,000	475,074
15	$100,000	2,688,805		100,000	615,329
16	$100,000	2,984,022		100,000	765,402
17	$100,000	3,299,903		100,000	925,980
18	$100,000	3,637,896		100,000	1,097,799
19	$100,000	3,999,549		100,000	1,281,645
20	$100,000	4,386,518		100,000	1,478,360
21	$100,000	4,800,574		100,000	1,688,845
22	$100,000	5,243,614		100,000	1,914,064
23	$100,000	5,717,667		100,000	2,155,049
24	$100,000	6,224,904		100,000	2,412,902
25	$100,000	6,767,647		100,000	2,688,805
26	$100,000	7,348,382		100,000	2,984,022
27	$100,000	7,969,769		100,000	3,299,903
28	$100,000	8,634,653		100,000	3,637,896
29	$100,000	9,346,079		100,000	3,999,549
30	$100,000	10,107,304		100,000	4,386,518
31	$100,000	10,921,815		100,000	4,800,574
32	$100,000	11,793,343		100,000	5,243,614
33	$100,000	12,725,876		100,000	5,717,667
34	$100,000	13,723,688		100,000	6,224,904
35	$100,000	14,791,346		100,000	6,767,647
36	$100,000	15,933,740		100,000	7,348,382
37	$100,000	17,156,102		100,000	7,969,769
38	$100,000	18,464,029		100,000	8,634,653
39	$100,000	19,863,511		100,000	9,346,079
40	$100,000	21,360,957		100,000	10,107,304
41	$100,000	22,963,224		100,000	10,921,815
42	$100,000	24,677,650		100,000	11,793,343
43	$100,000	**$26,512,085**		100,000	**$12,725,876**

Total Contributions	**$4,300,000**			**$3,300,000**	

THE GEOMETRIC JUMP

Compounding is actually pretty amazing. If you have a plan in mind over ten, twenty, thirty, or forty years, compounding works in a special way we call "geometric compounding." Let's say that a person starting from zero today has a twenty-five year wealth goal to be independent and calculates the amount of wealth needed to accomplish that (using the Wealth Building Formula®). There is going to be an amount that person must save each year at an assumed rate of return to reach that goal. The key is to get to geometric compounding. Geometric compounding works in a way that's very predictable—you can calculate it very easily—but because compounding starts off slowly and only gains a lot of steam way down the line, it can discourage you from saving or making the proper financial choice.

What do I mean by that? While compounding occurs from when you first begin to save, the real power of compounding that occurs in the later stage of your wealth building. If you diligently save what you are supposed to save annually, then you will reach geometric compounding about two-thirds of the way through the time frame of your financial plan. At this point, if you look at what you have accrued in wealth, you will see that you have about one-third of what you need to be financially independent.

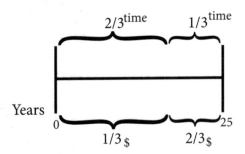

The first 2/3 that time passes, you only accumulate 1/3 of the dollars of wealth you need. The last 1/3 of the time you accumulate 2/3 of the wealth you need.

Imagine—it took you two-thirds of the years in your financial plan to get to grow only one-third of what you need! Makes you feel good, right? Probably not; if you hired workers to build a new home, and they asked for two-thirds of the money to build one-third of your house, would you agree to that? No, of course not. If you have paid them two-thirds of the money, you want the home project to be two-thirds done!

This is linear thinking. Money and wealth do not grow that way. So when you see two-thirds of time pass and you see only one-third of the wealth goal, you are not happy. You may think, *I have to make up two-thirds of my financial wealth goal, and I have only one-third of my time left.* Again, you may intellectually understand compounding, but emotionally, this does not feel good.

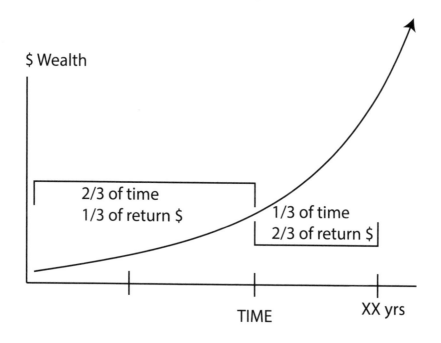

If you have saved faithfully, the "magic" of compounding occurs in the last one-third of the time, generating two-thirds of the returns.

You might think, *I am not going to make it.* When people think they're not going to make their financial goals, they tend to make poor financial choices. They make decisions like, "I'm not one of the chosen ones, so I might as well just spend it and enjoy life." Or they might decide, "I'm not getting enough return. My uncle knows this really great guy who guarantees a 50 percent rate of return per year. So if I really goose up my rate of return, maybe I can take on more risk and make up the time that I've lost." Folks, if it sounds too good to believe, it probably is. People who throw common sense to the wind and take inordinate risks lose money. If you just give compounding a chance, you will make it!

STICK WITH THE PLAN

Even though you're two-thirds through your allotted time and see that you're only saved a third of what you need, stick with it, because the magic of what we call the "geometric jump" happens in that last third of your financial plan. If I were to draw a line showing the progress of geometric compounding, the line would be relatively flat from year zero to about twelve, and then it would go up geometrically. If you stick with the plan and keep saving, it's during that last third that you actually make up more than two-thirds of the wealth that you need to achieve your goals. (See Compounding and "Geometric Jump" charts above.)

As I've said, people don't understand this, and even when it's explained, they don't believe it. Because of that, they make poor financial choices that prevent them from reaching that geometric jump or compounding adequately in the years they wish. I worked with a cardiology group in Dallas. Their practice was doing very well, but their personal cash flows were getting tight. They were reaching their late forties and early fifties, and most of them had kids in college, so they had other expenses bearing down on them. All of a sudden they couldn't save, even in their 401(k) or their pension plan.

They were working very hard and were really frustrated by that state of affairs, so they called us in.

The cardiologists had debt within their practice—about $5 million in equipment. Like most people, they were out to pay this debt down quickly, over about five years or less if they could. But what they weren't seeing was that the loan principal payments were hurting their practice's cash flow and decreasing their personal cash flows to the extent that they took home less and could not save in their pension plans. Getting them to renegotiate the debt with the bank and paying it off over ten years (the useful life of the equipment was up to fifteen years) instead of five loosened up a lot of cash flow in their practice. Now they could fund their pension plans, save on income taxes due to the pension plan deduction, and get back to compounding their wealth and achieving their goals in the time frame they wished.

Another client had a string of high-end boutique jewelry stores. They owned a couple of the buildings their stores were in, and they were renegotiating debt on these buildings for $8 million to pay off the debt on their other buildings over fifteen years. There were points and other bank fees they were paying that were costing them quite a lot, and they needed help. In line with our Integrated Cash Flow Management Approach℠, we said, "How can we find more investable cash?"

We met with the clients and their bankers and explained that we would like either an interest-only loan or a loan that could be amortized over thirty years. In the end, we were able to find investable cash of hundreds of thousands of dollars per year for our client due to the bank accepting a longer payout time period. They had the choice of putting this cash toward a pension plan (getting more investable cash due to tax savings), using it to expanding the business, or helping them build more wealth. At the same time, we were also able to renegotiate the fees they were paying for the loan, which saved them an additional tens of thousands of dollars. For them, knowing their Wealth Building Formula® and employing our Integrated Cash Flow Management Approach℠ allowed them to recognize an opportunity to get to geometric compounding sooner.

HOW DO I START TAKING ADVANTAGE OF COMPOUNDING?

What if you hit a rough patch with your career or in your business? Normally you would have to save $100,000 a year to achieve your financial goals, but maybe right now you can only save $50,000 or even less. The key is saving any amount you can as soon as possible (saving now versus later) and then targeting to save the rest when you can. Even if you start out saving $10,000 a year, knowing that you need to save $100,000 or more, you will eventually find a way to do that because now you have a target; before, you had no target at all. The sooner you begin, the further the power of compounding and getting to geometric compounding will take you.

But what's the best way to save your money while saving it from being depleted by taxes? We'll discuss that next.

CHAPTER SIX

THE TAX SAVING
SAVINGS EFFECT

You must pay taxes. But there's no law that
says you gotta leave a tip.
—Morgan Stanley

A key component to working your personal Wealth Building Formula® is understanding how the Tax Saving Savings Effect works. This is another way in which to find more investable cash or cash flow through our Integrated Cash Flow Management Approach℠ that allows you to save more money without working harder or longer.

Going back to the Wealth Building Formula®, if people have to save $100,000 a year and are able to do so, then they're going to be on track for the time frame in which they want to be independent. However, if we can find more investable cash and they decide to save that too, they'll get to their wealth building goal sooner; or have more wealth when they get there; or can reduce the risk of their portfolio. So how do we accomplish that?

Say that you have a few million dollars put away, but because of various expenses, you can't save any more than $50,000. You know that you have to save $100,000 a year to achieve your financial goals, but the only option you seem to have to achieve that is to work harder at your job. If you work harder in your businesses or for your employer, you could earn $30,000 more. At this point, you say, "I can save this additional $30,000. I'm going to put it in my savings account," and you're pleased because you feel that you've come close to your annual goal.

But have you? Between state and federal taxes, it's not hard to wind up in a 40 percent tax bracket. You just earned another $30,000, and 40 percent of that is $12,000, meaning that you have to come up with $12,000 in extra cash just to pay your taxes. You want to save at least the $30,000, but in order to pay your income taxes you would have to subtract $12,000 from the $30,000. Once you realize this, the question becomes, "How can I make up that missing $12,000?" The obvious choice is to work harder to make even more to cover that savings shortfall. So you decide to work harder and make that additional $12,000.

But now you have to pay 40 percent of that new $12,000—it is earned income—so you are still short of that elusive goal. You're getting closer, but it seems as though no matter how much work you pile on, that 40 percent tax bite undoes your efforts.

Tax Savings Savings Effect

(OR HOW TO TURN $30,000 INTO $50,000 WITHOUT WORKING HARDER)

$30,000 X 40%	=	$12,000
12,000 X 40%	=	4,800
4,800 X 40%	=	1,920
1,920 X 40%	=	768
768 X 40%	=	307
307 X 40%	=	123
123 X 40%	=	49
49 X 40%	=	20
20 X 40%	=	8
8 X 40%	=	3
3 X 40%	=	1
1 X 40%	=	.4
.40 X40%	=	.16

Totals (rounded up) $50,000 X 40% = $20,000

So, to save $30,000 (non tax sheltered), you must earn $50,000 and pay $20,000 in income taxes.

Having to earn $50,000 to net after tax to $30,000 makes sense since 40% of $50,000 equals taxes of $20,000.

The Tax Savings Savings Effect: If you begin to save the $30,000 in a tax sheltered way (i.e. pension), you reduce income taxes. If you save the tax savings, you can reverse the above and save $50,000 by initially saving $30,000.

The more money you earn, the more taxes you're going to pay. This is the tax effect. Per the illustration, you can see that you'll actually have to earn $50,000 to have that full $30,000 to save because if you earn $50,000 and are in a 40 percent tax bracket, your taxes on that will be $20,000.

BUT THERE'S GOOD NEWS

You can make taxes work for you, instead of against you, if you utilize what we call the "Tax Saving Savings Effect." Finding tax savings and then saving the investable cash from the Tax Saving Savings Effect has a big compounding effect on your wealth. Let's say you find a way to shelter your $30,000 from taxes so that you can make (or beat) your savings goal. One way is to contribute the extra earnings to a pension plan. Sheltering those earnings in a pension plan turns them from a tax liability into a tax deduction. The $30,000 is now subtracted from your taxable income rather than added to it. If you're earning $500,000 and you put this $30,000 into a pension plan, your taxable income is now only $470,000. So now, if you're saving 40 percent of $30,000, there's now $12,000 you effectively won't have to pay: either the government will refund you $12,000, or you can reduce your withholdings or quarterly tax payments by $12,000.

You now have $12,000 of "found money." You can either spend it or save it. If you save it, you will get to your financial goals sooner, have more cash flow or wealth when you get there, or reduce the risk in your portfolio.

The better financial choice is to take the $12,000 and also contribute that to your pension plan. If you save that money in your pension plan, you save 40 percent of $12,000 due to the tax deduction, which is $4,800. You can contribute that $4,800 to the pension plan, and you save 40 percent of that, which is $1,920.

Any person who begins saving $30,000 a year can actually save $50,000 a year if they save the tax savings that they were going to pay to the government. Accordingly, if you can save $300,000 in a pension plan, you can save $500,000 due to the Tax Saving Savings Effect. Two partners at a Midwest law firm we've consulted with were able to save $500,000 a year in their particular pension plan due to this strategy. You can imagine the cash flow effect they got from that: the government was paying for almost half of their pension contribution!

Recently, dealing with the five partners and sixty employees of a business, we were able to show them a pension plan where they could contribute almost $1 million per year and save almost $500,000 in taxes. Employee costs were $50,000 net of tax. For them, they could shelter almost $1 million to grow tax deferred, have the government pay about half of it, and have a net cost of $50,000 for their employees. This is the power of the Tax Saving Savings Effect.

Understanding the Tax Saving Savings Effect allows you to work your Wealth Building Formula® and, along with the power of compounding, to make the 100 percent correct financial choice to save more money without working one day longer.

THE KEY WORD IS "SMARTER"

Keep in mind that the power of understanding all of the concepts we have discussed so far is what I mean by the word smarter in "make smarter financial choices that don't require you to work harder or longer." Just by doing what I call "shuffling paper"—just filling out paperwork—you can utilize compounding and the Tax Saving Savings Effect to your advantage to grow your wealth in less time and with less work.

Life insurance can be another example: I had a business client who was paying a life insurance premium of $100,000, which is not a tax-deductible item; thus, because of the tax bite (assuming a 40 percent tax bracket), he actually had to earn $166,667 (40 percent of $166,667 equals $66,667 that would go to income tax) to get that $100,000 for the premium.

Suppose you could find a policy that protects you the same way but only costs you $40,000? Your savings before taxes is $60,000 ($100,000 less $40,000). Using the Tax Saving Savings Effect illustration and assuming you could place the $60,000 (and the tax savings on it) in a pension, your total savings after taxes is now $100,000. That means that with the same $100,000, if you could structure it this way, you could actually pay for your insurance for free and save the $100,000 per year.

When we talked about mortgages, we've only discussed the compounding effect: if you could pay less on your mortgage by having an interest-only mortgage or a longer payout, you could save that money and get to your wealth goals sooner. But there's something else to consider when you look at compounding: the Tax Saving Savings Effect.

Remember the example where you had $30,000 a year to save? Let's say that when you earned it, instead of saving it in your pension plan, you took the $30,000 and paid down more principal on your mortgage. When you earn this $30,000, you have to pay tax on it. When you contribute the $30,000 to a pension, it becomes a tax deduction and you do not pay tax on it. Because paying principal is not a tax deduction, paying the $30,000 toward the principal of the mortgage instead of contributing to your pension, you have to pay $20,000 in taxes. This means that every time you pay principal of $30,000 on your mortgage, you have to go out and actually earn

$50,000—$20,000 to pay your taxes and $30,000 to pay the bank. If you do this, put yourself in the position of paying more in taxes, which takes away from your *C* (wealth) and means taking more time to get to geometric compounding.

The savvy way to use the compounding and Tax Saving Savings Effect in that example is to take that $30,000, contribute this amount to your pension plan, and save the tax savings of $20,000 or a total of $50,000 per year. How many people do you know who pay extra on their mortgage each month? Doing this blindly is what I call being "anti-geometric." If you fail to use the power of compounding or of the Tax Saving Savings Effect, you can wind up having less wealth and thus less cash flow, having to earn more money in your investment portfolio during the life of your portfolio, thereby having to increase risk or having to work longer or harder.

HOW TO MAKE IT WORK IN YOUR FAVOR

"All right, Al, I found all this extra investable cash. How can I use compounding and tax savings to the maximum?"

There's a priority in where you're going to save money, and the first priority is trying to get the most compounding you can. Normally, you do this by putting it in the most tax-sheltered, tax-advantageous account you can. That means putting your investable cash savings in a tax-advantaged or tax-shelter account where not only are you getting a tax deduction but the money also is growing tax deferred, so you're not paying tax on the earnings. That account could be a savings plan like a 401(k), which is also called a *defined contribution plan*; a pension plan or deferred compensation plan at work; or, if you have a business, a 401(k), a cash balance plan, or a *defined benefit plan*. Any of these would be your first and best choices.

If you can't put your money where you can receive a tax deduction, the second choice is to put it into an account in which it will at least be growing tax deferred, like an IRA or maybe some sort of insurance vehicle.

A side note on IRAs: as you grow older, you may get to a point when you can have these IRAs rolled over into a Roth IRA. A Roth IRA allows you to take out these monies tax-free in the future or to pass them on to the next generation, who may not have to pay the tax on the earnings. It's not as advantageous as the first choice—your 401(k) or pension plan—but it's a good second choice if it's what's available to you.

The last choice is to put your savings into a taxable account. This is just a bank account or an investment account that offers you no tax advantage. You've already paid the taxes on this money, and you will pay the tax on the earnings. People normally save in all three categories: tax-advantaged, tax-deferred, and taxable accounts.

Another place to put money is in real estate. You can buy real estate and get a mortgage on it. As it grows in value, that value (equity) will grow, tax deferred. You're only going to pay taxes on it when you sell it. When that real estate is sold, you get another tax advantage called capital gains treatment, which is normally taxed at a lower percentage than ordinary income. Another nice aspect of real estate is that sometimes, if you're purchasing it through corporations or other entities, you can get tax deductions that help to shelter other income.

Another great option with real estate investment is that you can take money from the equity you have built by borrowing from it. You don't pay taxes on this. This can allow you to take advantage of compounding and the Tax Saving Savings Effect. I had a client who was a retired executive of a Fortune 500 company; he had a net worth of $15 million, $5 million of which was in two pieces of real estate. His primary residence was in Florida so that he did not have to pay state income taxes, but he liked to go visit his children and stay at his second home outside of Florida. The real estate was debt-free, and he was living a good life off of the $10 million he had in liquid investments.

As the client and his wife got into their early seventies, cash flow became a little tighter. That $10 million in liquid assets started to shrink, as did the cash flow it generated. He came to us and said, "I need to bolster my cash flow, but I don't know how to get access to more assets to generate more cash flow without selling one or both of the properties, which I don't really want to do."

Because he had previously created a financial plan with us, we knew his Wealth Building Formula® and made this recommendation to him: "You have $5 million of real estate, which you own outright. Given today's low-interest-rate environment, why don't you borrow $2.5 million from your real estate, which is about half of what its value is? In effect you're borrowing this at about a 3 percent rate, and you've been earning 6 percent or more on your portfolio. If you take this $2.5 million out and put it into your portfolio, you will earn the difference between the 6 percent you've been earning on average and the 3 percent that you're paying on the mortgage—so you will net an extra 3 percent."

Three percent of $2.5 million equals $75,000, so this client was going to increase his cash flow by $75,000 per year before tax—not by working harder, not by going back to work, just by "shuffling paper." But even on an after-tax basis he actually made out even better than that because he was able to deduct the interest for that mortgage on his tax return.

Leveraging the Equity in Your Home to Create Investable Cash

TAKE OUT A $2.5 MILLION MORTGAGE AT 3%, INVEST IT FOR RETURNS OF 6%.

INCOME		
	$150,000	Income earned from investing
Less	$45,000	Income taxes on the income (blended cap gains and ordinary rates)
Net Income	$105,000	
COST		
	$75,000	3% interest on $2.5 million mortgage
Less	$13,200	Possible tax savings on deducting interest (($1.1 million x 3%) x 40%)
Net Cost	$61,800	
INCOME - COST		
	$ 43,200	Possible Net Investable Cash Created

There are limitations to how much you can deduct on mortgages, but in this case he could deduct a little less than half of the interest. With that deduction, and in his bracket, he was no longer paying a 3 percent rate. He was paying closer to a 2.5 percent rate or less, further increasing his cash flow. Again, just by using the Tax Saving Savings Effect and compounding, we were able to come up with a solution that allowed him to increase his cash flow.

You might say, "He had to pay tax on the amount of earnings he had in his portfolio," and that's true. But there are strategies that we'll discuss later that mean you don't have to pay the full tax rate on the amount you're earning on investments. He could have sold one of his homes. Let's say one of his homes was worth that $2.5 million; he could have sold the home and paid taxes on the gains. But by borrowing the $2.5 million, he did not have a taxable event. He could actually take that money from the real estate, not pay any taxes on it, invest it, and stretch out his cash flow and his wealth to last his lifetime and his spouse's.

CHAPTER SEVEN

FINDING MORE INVESTABLE CASH—IMAGINATION

Logic will take you from A to B.
Imagination will take you everywhere.
—Albert Einstein

How do you envision the life you want for yourself, now and in the future? Maybe you want to have great vacations, to have a great vacation home, or to be able to travel by private jet. If you're unable to live the way you wish, no matter how much you're saving toward financial independence, it makes that saving a much harder chore. People want to have choices as to whether they continue to work or to do something else. We at Traust Sollus believe that they should.

Our Integrated Cash Flow Management Approach℠, coupled with our Wealth Management Formula® process, maps a clear path to achieving these life goals. It's the same with companies and your personal finances: the better financial choices you make, the more you're going to have now and for life. Poor choices will sentence you to working harder in life or not having the options you want.

WHAT ARE YOUR BENCHMARKS?

We've discussed the process and methodology to making smart choices and the fact that so many people lack the know-how or tools that businesses use to make those good financial decisions for themselves. Businesses have benchmarks that can be compared to other companies in the same industry.

Most individuals don't have these benchmarks. The most you can do is to look at how much you have in the bank or your investment accounts or if your investments did better than the S&P 500 for the last quarter or year. But you don't know how to bring it all together; you don't have a road map to tell you where you are or a whole view of your finances like a well-run company would.

We've talked through the principle of compounding as a key to achieving your Wealth Building Formula®, which says that if you save now rather than later, you're going to have more. If you wait to save until later, you're going to have less wealth and cash flow. Harnessing the power of compounding sounds simple, but people just don't do it. Most decisions they make are meant to save later rather than now because while they intellectually understand compounding, emotionally they don't believe it. People think linearly, and compounding is an geometric calculation.

We've also discussed another thing critical to your Wealth Building Formula®, which is understanding the Tax Saving Savings Effect—making the right choices around taxes and finding more investable cash by paying less to the government.

So what does all this mean? When you make uninformed financial decisions, whether it's because you're in a hurry or you don't really understand the ramifications, you can wind up creating a sort of financial domino effect that affects you in ways you don't foresee and eventually leads to you having less cash flow than you need. I chose to be a wealth advisor because I wanted to transform lives in the way that having this knowledge transformed mine. As a baker's son, I'd grown up in a profession in which most people worked until they were seventy or older. I saw that I could help other people make better financial choices so they could have the same thing that I eventually achieved: to be financially independent by age forty-eight and able to do whatever I wished in life beyond that.

Every decision that you make in your financial life—whether it's going out to dinner, deciding to buy an insurance policy, buying or leasing a car, paying down a mortgage faster, hiring more employees, expanding your operation, buying another business, or buying more equipment—is going to have an effect on your Wealth Building Formula®, your current and future cash flow, and the way you will live now and in the future. Let's say you make a decision that increases your cash flow, and you decide to save the excess cash flow; again, you can get to your wealth goals quicker, add more wealth when you get there, or reduce the risk in your investment portfolio. Of those three choices, what I find that most people find the most attractive among them is "getting to your wealth goals quicker" or what I refer to as "saving years of life."

SAVING YEARS OF LIFE

Millionaires or multimillionaires may not have enough wealth to be financially independent, but they're well on their way. But I've seen many a millionaire mess up. They'll be enjoying a smooth sail on the fair winds of a healthy economy, and then suddenly, they get swamped by a big wave. The market tanks, the real estate environment changes, their business is out of sync, or maybe their employer lets them go. Without warning and even though they have some wherewithal, they're not going to have enough to live the life they wish, now or in the future. See my above comment on the *New York Times* article "Reversal of Fortune for Some Superrich."

When I offer people the options of becoming financially independent sooner, having more wealth when they get there, or reducing the risk in their portfolio, most people say, "I'd like to retire sooner," or, "I'd like to be independent sooner." That said, it's my observation that well over 90 percent of the people I've dealt with do not stop working and play golf for the rest of their lives. The vast majority continues to work because they like what they do; hold onto their business because they like their business; or do something else that is challenging, enjoyable, or a contribution to society.

For example, I had a client, Sally, who was the owner of a small chain of restaurants and had done very well. She had just turned fifty, and now sixty didn't look that far off. Did she really want to keep working after sixty?

We sat down together and went through a comprehensive personal financial plan with her that encompassed what she wanted in life, what her cash flow was, and all the things we've talked about in earlier chapters. We made sure that she had her own customized Wealth Building Formula®. All she really wanted to know was whether she was going to be okay to retire by the time she was sixty or sixty-five. She was living a pretty good lifestyle; she wanted to get a second home and travel more, but she wasn't sure she could afford that. But it was more important for her to know that, somewhere along the way, she was going to have options and not have to work.

We said, "Sally, we don't think that you're going to have a problem retiring by sixty-five. If you sell your business at the price you need, you could retire closer to sixty."

She said she wanted to live a better lifestyle now rather than later. So we dug into ways that we could improve her cash flow, and we showed her that not only could she have that vacation home now but that it was very possible for her to be financially independent years earlier than age sixty. Sometimes, by using your imagination and partnering with someone, you can find the answers. One of the problems is that many people do not take the time to ponder, explore, or create with their trusted advisor.

Sally is now in her sixties and still owns her restaurants—although by about age fifty-seven, she no longer needed to work. Realizing that she didn't have to work changed her whole view about the stress and anxiety of running a business. Suddenly, without the pressure, it became more enjoyable to her—more like a game. She was eager to take risks and try new experiences she wouldn't have considered before. She even started a foundation. That's the power of having a plan and taking the time to work on the business, not just in the business.

One client couple I worked with, Bob and Carol, were both executives. In the course of sitting down with them, they revealed that although they both liked their careers, they were each interested in doing something different with their lives. Bob confided that he'd always wanted to be a writer of science fiction. He wanted to take writing courses and see if he could turn out some short stories or a book, but the time demands of his career made that impossible. Carol wanted to be more active in the community and turn her talents to volunteering or to teaching underprivileged children, particularly those with special needs. Bob and Carol were in their midforties when they came to see me; they're presently in their midfifties, and thanks to their dedication to working their Wealth Building Formula®, they're within a couple of years of achieving their respective goals.

Use your imagination. Dream of the life you want. Then find out how to make better financial choices and become fully aware of the impact those choices will have on your financial well-being. That's the path to making those dreams your reality: making a conscious choice.

CHOOSE ON PURPOSE, NOT BY DEFAULT

Among my clients was a gentleman who had a strong desire to fund a scholarship. He could have retired sooner had he chosen to invest the $50,000 per year that he was putting toward funding this scholarship, but as he told me, "I would prefer to take my time and to take a little longer to get to retirement but to also know I could make a difference along the way." People want to be able to make prudent financial decisions, to achieve certain things or options in their life and also to live the way they want to along the way.

Most people want to save time, though, as I said earlier. By finding additional investable cash, you're saving years of life—years in which you would otherwise have had to work. You get to your options sooner rather than later. Because they don't have a clear way in which to make a better choice, however, many people make choices that mean getting to their goals will take longer or that they'll fail to amass the wealth or the cash flow that they need.

Remember, every financial choice, no matter how small, can have a big impact on your ability to get where you want to go sooner. No financial choice exists in a vacuum, and that certainly includes choices about debt, which we'll cover in depth in the next chapter.

CHAPTER EIGHT

USING DEBT SMARTER— THE TRUTH ABOUT DEBT AND WEALTH CREATION

Opportunities multiply as they are seized.
—Sun Tzu

I've talked a little about how, in my experience, most people fear debt; they've absorbed the teachings of their parents or the pundits who say that when you get a chance to pay off debt, you want to do that first, as quickly as possible, and *then* save. Certainly, they say, by the time you reach your retirement years, you want the house paid off and no debt hanging over your head.

People say these things because most people feel really good about the idea of being debt-free. There's an emotional kick to knowing that you don't owe anyone anything, so people take that emotion and equate it with success. It becomes a yardstick: "How can I go into retirement with a mortgage? I'm not successful if I couldn't pay off my debt, right?" People are obsessed about this, and the root source of that anxiety isn't hard to identify if you have even a nodding acquaintance with twentieth-century history: the Great Depression.

THE GRAPES OF WRATH MIND-SET

Many of us have either parents or grandparents who lived through the Great Depression. The Great Depression scarred anyone who came through it. It was a time in which people lost their homes, jobs, businesses, and dignity. My father was in his early teens during the Great Depression, and he told me horror stories. My grandfather lost his bakery in the Midwest because of the Great Depression. My father remembered waking up every day to find my grandfather, who'd been up since dawn, making dough and frying doughnuts in a cauldron of boiling fat on the stove of their kitchen. My father would help him put the doughnuts on paper on the floor to cool, and then they would sugar the doughnuts. They'd put them in paper containers, and my father and his brother and sisters would go door to door, selling them for a few cents each. My father remembers graduating in bare feet from eighth grade. Until the day he died, whenever my father told that story, it was with such emotion and such hurt that you could almost feel like you were that little boy whose graduation day was stained with the shame of not having shoes.

My grandfather could not keep up with his family's rent; my father remembers the day that the landlord came to the door of the house they were renting and told them that they had to get out, right then. They couldn't take their belongings; all they could do was to get in their car and drive away. They had to leave everything behind: their clothes, their furniture—my father even had to leave his dog behind, another thing that scarred his memory forever. They made their way to the East Coast, to Philadelphia, where eventually they got back on their feet.

My father certainly believed that debt was bad, and he never wanted to owe anyone anything. If he couldn't pay cash for something, he didn't buy it. He only bought used cars for cash, and he would never get loans. He never had a credit card. Only one time did he have a mortgage, when he owned a small row home in Philadelphia. The mortgage payment was less than $40 per month. He fell behind on some payments once, sold the house, and rented forever after. Debt was bad.

Experiences like these, all too common during the Great Depression and during tough financial times, gave birth to what I call "the *Grapes of Wrath* mentality." It's linked to what happened in the Midwest farming belt. Most farmers had little or no debt on their farms. Then a great drought created the Dust Bowl. If they had little or no debt, farmers couldn't pay their property taxes and lost their farms. Ironically, those farmers who had more debt but also more savings did fine. They had the reserves to weather the downturn. Farmers who did not lost their properties.

It wasn't only the Depression that created hardship and loss; a bank president told me a story about some rental houses his family had owned during World War II. They didn't have any debt on the houses, but because it was wartime, the government set rent limits on them and set them very low. The rents weren't sufficient to cover his parents' costs in upkeep or property taxes, and they eventually had to give away the properties. His parents didn't have the wealth to send him to college, and he had to work his way through school. Why? In part because his parents didn't have the cash reserves to weather the downturn and retain their wealth.

I am telling you these stories to establish the way in which we think about debt and why we think that way. We are told stories about past generations losing property or having financial difficulty, and we associate that with debt: if only they had not had that debt, they would have been okay. But if they had maintained some level of debt to have reserves when times were bad, like a well-run company, they most likely would have been all right. The lesson to be learned here is about using debt smarter.

To pay off debt principal, you must earn money. When you earn money, you have to pay taxes on it. When you pay those taxes, you have to earn more than what you pay to the bank or mortgage company for your debt, so you have to work harder to do that (the Tax Saving Savings Effect). Because of the way tax laws are structured, paying down debt faster means losing that interest deduction sooner. Thus you find yourself paying more taxes and end up saving your money later, violating both the principle of compounding and the Tax Saving Savings Effect.

During a white-collar recession we experienced in the mid-1980s, many companies had to lay off a lot of their management or white-collar workers. AT&T had a very large operation in our local area, and they too laid off a lot of executives. Many of these executives came to us for advice. These were people who were accustomed to being able to afford a nice life. They had homes in the area that were very expensive. Most of them were probably in their late forties to midfifties. They had built up their lifestyle to match their salary in a way that left little room for savings. They hadn't expected to get laid off, and suddenly they were faced with maintaining an expensive lifestyle without the resources to do so. They did have some savings in their 401(k)s and some stock options (which were now worth less), but they had very little outside of those assets that they could draw on to support them. Most of them had small or no mortgages; they had paid them off quickly but had not saved reserves. Having little or no income, some paid their mortgages payments from their

401(k)s until there was little or nothing left. Once they exhausted their 401(k)s, what happened? They had to sell their homes at fire-sale prices.

BE PREPARED FOR THE WORST, AND IT WON'T BE AS BAD

We could help these executives to a certain degree, but the best advice I would give you is to avoid putting yourself in that position in the first place. Start planning well ahead of time for a potential recession or job loss. Suppose that there were two people, each of whom buys a house for one million dollars. Each of them also has one million dollars in investments. One of these people hates debt, so he takes that million dollars and pays off his mortgage. He now owns the house free and clear. The other homebuyer asks for our advice, and we recommend to her, "Take out a mortgage for as much as possible to preserve the cash you have in your investment account. You will have this money in the event of an emergency, it will continue to grow wealth by compounding, and you will receive extra investable cash by having the interest as a tax deduction." Let's further assume that both of these people suddenly lose their jobs. What choices do both have? He has a million-dollar house he owns free and clear, and she has a $600,000 mortgage and $600,000 in investments. They're both good executives, so they're likely to get jobs at some point in the future. But in a down cycle of the economy, it might take a long time to find a new job, or they may have to relocate to find employment. The process may take six months, a year, or even longer.

The person who had the paid-off, free-and-clear house made what he felt was a safe and wise choice. But now he doesn't have cash flow coming in. He has to feed his family and pay for heat, light, home insurance, and property taxes. What options does a person with a million-dollar house and no other assets have? He may go to the bank to which he'd paid his mortgage and ask for a home equity loan, but because he has no cash flow, no job, and no liquid assets, he's unlikely to get it.

Another choice might be to put his house on the market in hopes of a fast sale, which may mean that he'll have difficulty selling it for the price he wants. A recession is the worst time to sell your house because other people may be in the same boat, which means that a lot of people are flooding the market with homes. But our debt-free person needs cash quickly, so he has to sacrifice the price he gets, maybe letting his house go for far less than it's actually worth.

What about our other laid-off executive, also a homeowner? Remember, she took our advice on taking out a $600,000 mortgage rather than paying for the house outright. That means she still has $600,000 in cash or investments that she can use. Her job situation is tough—she still has to find work—but in the meantime, her money is generating cash flow (interest, dividends, or capital gains) to cover her expenses, and she has access to the assets. She's far more likely to be able to weather this storm. But she has other options: If she goes to the bank for a home equity loan, having a comfortable cushion of investments makes it far likelier that she'll get that loan.

Finally, she will not have to sell the house and sacrifice its value. Even if she eventually has to move to another city or state, she can take her time to get the highest possible value for the property. The person who has no accessible liquid assets and no debt has few or no options. The person who has accessible liquid assets and debt has many options.

DEBT DECISION #1	
Assumptions: • Both have $1 million of liquid investments or cash. • Both wish to buy a house for $1 million.	
PERSON A	**PERSON B**
1. Puts down $1 million for house 2. Has no mortgage (or cash left)	1. Puts down $400,000 for house 2. Obtains a $600,000 mortgage and invests the $600,000 left over from the $1 million
Both A and B lose their jobs in a recession. • Who has more options? • Who is safer? • Who is taking advantage of compounding and The Tax Savings Savings Effect? • Who will probably achieve their financial goals first? • Who will work longer and harder in their life?	

Let's examine another hypothetical that relates to the idea of debt but that also illustrates how you can put yourself behind in your financial plan with a lack of understanding of the principal of compounding. You're building wealth well, but you're only about a third of the way to your financial goal. You have a home that's worth $1 million. You have a $500,000 mortgage on it. Then, this house across town that you've always loved and wanted to buy comes up for sale for $2 million. You decide, "I have $3 million in investment accounts, and I have worked diligently for years. I'm going to buy that house!"

DEBT DECISION #2
Assumptions: • Both have $3 million of liquid investments or cash. • Both have a house worth $1 million. • Both have a current mortgage of $500,000. • Both wish to buy a house for $2 million. • Both have cash flow to pay for a $1.5 million mortgage. **What mortgage should they have if they wish to get to geometric compounding and achieve financial independence in the shortest time?**
PERSON A
1. Sells current home and pays off mortgage of $500,000 2. Buys new home and places $500,000 from the sale of the previous home on the new home 3. Takes $1.5 million from savings to pay for the home 4. Has $1.5 million left in savings
PERSON B
1. Sells current home and pays off mortgage of $500,000 2. Buys new home and places $500,000 from the sale of the previous home on the new home 3. Takes out a $1.5 million mortgage 4. Maintains $3 million in savings
RESULTS
• Person A falls below or further from geometric compounding. • Person A does not take advantage of compounding or Tax Savings Savings Effect. • Person A will take longer to achieve their financial goals. • Person A will have to work harder and longer.

So you sell your $1 million house, pay off the mortgage, and put the $500,000 you get from the sale down on the new house. Now you have a financial choice to make: you can take out a $1.5 million mortgage (three times the mortgage you had before); you can take another $1 million from your investment accounts, put that down on the house, and have the same $500,000 mortgage you had before; or you could take $1.5 million and pay off the house completely.

What would most people do? What would you do? Because of this obsession with being out of debt, especially by the time they're retired or independent, most would pay down more of the mortgage or maybe even the whole thing. However, if you remember the principal of compounding and are working your Wealth Building Formula®, you know that when you take money away from your investable wealth, you have less money that's going to compound, and it will take you more time to achieve the "geometric jump." If you replace that wealth through saving, you will eventually get to the powerful part of compounding, what we referred to as "geometric" compounding, but it will take more years of life and more years of having to go to that office and work.

Yet people make this kind of choice based on the emotional dread of debt without realizing the effects on their financial lives. It is not difficult to see how this choice affects you. It is a matter of "running the numbers"—doing the calculations to see how this choice affects you. But people just don't take the time to do this. Companies and people have the same choices around debt as in the examples here. You have some companies that start on a shoestring, don't plan cash flow properly, and don't have the cash reserves, and when something happens, there's nothing to fall back on. They can have a great business and actually be profitable, but their cash flow is poor, and they go under. Other companies start off by prudently planning debt, ensuring that they will have reserves for unforeseen events. They have a better chance of making it because they planned debt and created shareholder wealth from it. It is exactly the same with individuals.

Over the years, I've given a lot of lectures to business and professional groups as well as to professionals who are just graduating. Many of these graduates, especially physicians, have up to $200,000 of student loan debt, and they leave school determined to pay it off in a three- to seven-year time frame just so they can get that "monkey" off their back. What I explain to these young physicians is that there are financial institutions that will let them pay this debt off over twenty-five years and that it might be a better financial choice if they are out to achieve financial independence in the shortest time frame. Let's explore why that's so.

As an example, you could pay off your $200,000 worth of loans over five years. That is about $44,000 per year (assuming a 5 percent rate of interest). If you financed $200,000 over twenty-five years instead, assuming a 5 percent interest rate, your annual payments with interest would be a little less than $14,000 per year. That means you save $30,000 ($44,000 – $14,000 = $30,000) of cash flow per year by extending the loans. If you're one of these young physicians and you joined a practice with a 401(k) or a pension plan, you could shelter that entire amount from income tax. Using the Tax Saving Savings Effect, this means that the total amount you could save (assuming a 40 percent tax rate) would be $50,000 (40% x $50,000 = $20,000 and $30,000 + $20,000 = $50,000). Saving $50,000 per year, tax deferred and assuming a growth rate of 6 percent, equals a bit more than $2.9 million over those twenty-five years. Did you have to work any harder for this $2.9 million? No. For some, this choice could fund one-third to one-half of their retirement cash flow!

Some might argue that getting the loans out of the way first and then saving the $44,000 per year might be better. Tell me, when you paid off a car loan, did you subsequently save the monthly amount of that payment? People don't tend to do this. Look back at my "Power of Compounding" illustration, and ask yourself which is better to be: the Go-Getter or the Slowpoke?

MAKE DEBT WORK FOR YOU, RATHER THAN AGAINST YOU

Whether it's paying off your student loans, mortgages, or the debts in your business, the choices you make are going to affect your Wealth Building Formula®. This in turn will affect how long you have to work, how much wealth you have when you decide to retire, and how much risk you must have in your investment portfolio.

I had a client who was starting out in her career, had $40,000 in loans, and owned a house with $200,000 in equity. She said that she wanted to start saving but could not. She wanted to pay off her loans over the next five years, and then she'd save.

"You have a house and you have some equity in it," I told her. "Your loans are $40,000. Why don't you just take out a home equity loan and pay off the loans now so that you can start saving those monthly payments right now into your 401(k) at work?"

How would this work to her advantage? She was paying about $1,700 a month for the loans. Immediately, she could start to save a lot more because a home equity payment cost only $333 per month. She could now save $1,367 ($1,700 − $333 = $1,367) per month or $16,404 per year. She would have contributions to place in her 401(k) and get tax benefits (via the Tax Saving Savings Effect) of an additional $10,936 (40% x $27,340 = $10,936) and could contribute a total of $27,340 per year to her 401(k) or tax-deferred plan. If she did this over thirty years, assuming a growth rate of 6 percent, she could have a total of almost $2.3 million, all by simply "shuffling paper," not by working an hour longer. This loan payment strategy was a multimillion-dollar decision that worked powerfully in her favor. It should be noted that if you are going to use debt smarter, you must save the difference to get the real benefit. If you are not, then you might as well pay down the debt.

When you're looking at debt as a way to create wealth, remember: saving now rather than later means that you'll take advantage of the principal of compounding. If you really do want to pay off your debt eventually, pay it off when you don't need to save anymore or at the end of your plan. Most people pay their debt down quickly at the beginning, which sentences them to work longer and harder. If you believe in the principal of compounding and the Tax Saving Savings Effect, that is how—and when—you pay off debt.

As I've noted, people do it the exact opposite way—to pay debt off quicker. They'll put an extra month's payment on their mortgage every year. They'll pay an extra few hundreds or thousands of dollars a month to get that debt down. That is against the principle of compounding and the Tax Saving Savings Effect—it makes your taxes higher and you end up having to work longer and harder. So why would you?

DON'T BE CAUGHT IN DEPRESSION-ERA IDEAS

Make your relationship with debt a healthy one, with you in the driver's seat. Don't let your attitudes toward it be dictated by emotions, what you've been told in the past, or a Depression-era mind-set. Most people don't use debt smarter because they don't have a way to make better financial decisions. If you know your Wealth Building Formula® and understand the power of compounding and of the Tax Saving Savings Effect, you have the option of using debt smarter to get to your goals faster, have more wealth when you get there, or reduce the risk in your investment portfolio, without having to work one day longer in life.

CHAPTER NINE

OTHER WAYS TO FIND INVESTABLE CASH

Money is better than poverty, if only for financial reasons.
—Woody Allen

We've already seen how finding more investable cash can move you toward your goals more quickly. But how and where can you most easily find it?

One of the first places you should look is at your own spending. Our philosophy around personal financial planning and spending is that you should live life the way you wish and not have to scrape to preserve, manage, or add to your wealth to get to your financial goals. But there are some meaningful ways to cut your spending without sacrificing your quality of life—in fact, you won't feel it at all.

IT HAPPENS WHEN YOU'RE NOT LOOKING

The fact is that people get very busy and consequently do things, which wastes cash flow that would otherwise be there for their lifestyle or for adding to their wealth. A good starting point to reclaiming this waste is to look at the arrangements that you might have, such as the personal services contracts or retainer fees you're paying companies, attorneys, or other experts. We had a client couple that had both an attorney and a consultant on retainer but really never used them. By changing that, they were able to save around $50,000 a year.

Many of our clients are wine connoisseurs; sometimes they'll tour the Napa Valley or other wine-producing regions, and they join wine clubs. They have it charged to their credit cards, and they don't keep track of it. All of a sudden, they're spending literally thousands of dollars a month on wine. They have so much wine coming in that it's often never taken out of the shipping cases. If that's you, it might be time to take a second look at that expenditure.

Even small things can add up when you take the power of compounding and the Tax Saving Savings Effect into consideration. A lot of people, personally or in business, will subscribe to periodicals or magazines, spending hundreds of dollars a month but never really looking at them. This may seem small, but with the power of compounding, it could be a multimillion-dollar decision! Many people have two, three, or even more homes, and they find that it's hard to visit all of them; they may feel that they can't take a vacation somewhere else, because they feel bound to use their homes. Do you really need that extra home? If you sold one, you might take trips to other places and spend less by renting instead of maintaining that home.

People will use their credit cards and not pay them off in a timely fashion. This can cost thousands of dollars. They have the cash flow, yet they incur a lot of unnecessary and avoidable charges by ignoring the payment due dates. Some of these are specialty cards that charge you up to $400 or $500 a year to be a cardholder. Do you really need that added card and expense? Maybe not. Yes, these are relatively small amounts, but remember compounding and the Tax Saving Savings Effect.

CHECK YOUR RATES

A simple way to keep track of your cash flow and where it's going is to make sure that every once in a while, you and your financial expert are looking at your credit card interest rates and balances. Maybe having your credit cards' balances refinanced into your home equity would save you money. What about the loan on your home or vacation home? Can you do better? Even if you have a business, having business loans refinanced can sometimes save thousands if not tens of thousands of dollars. We recently saved a business more than $100,000 a year in investable cash on negotiating rates and payouts.

A client was in the office just recently; we had asked her a few times to give us the information on her sizable mortgage, but she'd gotten busy and neglected to do so. When she finally got around to it, we discovered that she was paying about 5 percent, much more than she should have been. Refinancing saved her tens of thousands a year.

OTHER WAYS TO FIND CASH FLOW

What are some other places where you might find more investable cash? As we discussed earlier, we encourage executives to review their company benefits programs to make certain they're taking full advantage of them, like being sure to fill up their 401(k)—especially if there's a company match. Is there a deferred bonus system? A deferred compensation plan at work could potentially help you to save tens of thousands if not hundreds of thousands of dollars a year. Are there stock options plans that you're not invested in? Are there free or low-cost life and disability insurance programs? When it comes to life insurance, sometimes an employer plan allows you to pay less through group coverage than if you were to buy life insurance outside of the group. The same benefit can extend to either disability insurance or long-term care. Sometimes employers don't offer these benefits, and of course if you change employers, you may lose some of these, but you may find that going to another employer will garner the same or greater benefits.

Again, what I'm talking about here is just shuffling paper, not working one hour longer or any harder. It's just a matter of looking at the day-to-day financial choices you're making and choosing to make better ones.

What are some other ways to find investable cash? When you're dealing with your current employer, discuss what the future holds. What does your position look like in two, five, or ten years? What's the opportunity for growth, not only in terms of promotion or position but in your compensation and any other benefits that you could get? Is it possible to structure your compensation in some other way? We've had some high-level executives who were getting toward the end of their careers, but their employers still found them extremely valuable. They structured new positions for themselves as independent contractors or consultants. They actually made more money—30 to 40 percent more cash flow in some cases—because the employer did not have to pay for all the benefits they'd had to before. As a self-employed contractor, you might be eligible to start your own pension plan and have access to myriad other ways to shelter your income than you could not as an employee. You might qualify for a home office tax deduction along with other business expense deductions that you couldn't take before leading you to more investable cash.

If you've been a successful executive at a company, you may want to investigate how valuable you could be to someone else. It doesn't have to be a competitor; it can be an employer that has a need for someone in the same position as yours, perhaps in a different industry. Remember that executive I talked about earlier, who wound up renegotiating her compensation package with her current employer because she'd taken the time to look around and discover other potential jobs? By bringing these to her employer's attention, she was able to increase her own compensation and opportunities and to achieve her goals sooner.

FINDING CASH FLOW IN YOUR BUSINESS

What if you're a business owner; what are some ways to find investable cash there? Sometimes, even though some firms will have a 401(k) plan, they're not fully funding it. Sometimes there's the misperception that you can't have a 401(k) plan and also fund an IRA, which is not true. Especially for small businesses, see if you can have what's called a *defined benefit plan* or, more common today, a cash balance plan.

We worked with two business owners in the Midwest; their firm had about twenty employees. The owners both made good money in their company, but they only had 401(k)s. With our help, they put together a cash balance pension plan and eventually were able to save another $200,000 each ($400,000) in their pension plan, which in their tax bracket (between federal and state was almost 50 percent) saved almost $200,000 (50% x $400,000 = $200,000) in income taxes. These tax savings paid for half of the $400,000 they put away in the pension plan! So the government helped them fund their pensions!

As we said earlier, we were looking at a sixty-person business that had six partners. We were able to advise the partners that they could put away almost another $1 million of their own compensation into a cash balance pension plan. Due to federal and state tax rates of almost 50 percent, they would save $500,000 of tax savings by funding this pension. This is not unusual!

As a business owner, when was the last time you took a serious look at your operating costs? How effective are your billing department and your accounts receivable policies? Sometimes you get sloppy in those areas, so you don't collect in a timely fashion. That carelessness can cost you tens if not hundreds of thousands of dollars in cash flow.

Are you charging enough for your services? We worked with a popular and successful executive coach who was working all kinds of hours. But he didn't seem to be able to make his financial plan work in terms of living the lifestyle he wanted to, paying his taxes, and putting aside what he had to save to eventually achieve his financial independence within the time frame he wanted. We sat down with him and said, "Why don't you double your prices? Instead of charging $7,500 a day, why not charge $15,000 a day?"

Of course, at first he was shocked by this idea. What would his clients think?

We said, "Well, why don't you test it? Test it on a new client, since you're already very busy."

He did that, and to his surprise, he found out that it had very little impact. If anything, just by charging more for his time, he was able to dramatically increase his income without raising his expenses or working longer hours. Again, he was "shuffling paper," not working harder.

Small businesses need to have clear earnings targets. Imagine if Apple's Tim Cook announced that he had no idea what their earnings would be in an upcoming quarter; their stockholders would not be pleased. Another thing we find often with small businesses is that they don't have budgets. We think this is a critical thing for a firm.

Another mistake businesses often make is failing to check their benefits packages for their employees often enough. If you're the owner of a small business and you offer health insurance, long-term care, life insurance, or any other type of benefit, it's important to have your packages reviewed at least once every two years, if not once a year. Again, we do this on a regular basis with our business clients. I can think of more than a few examples where clients have saved tens or hundreds of thousands of dollars (depending on the size of their operations). Not only that, sometimes they're even able to enhance the benefits they provide. I'm not suggesting that employers decrease their employees' benefits, but by pointing out that products and offerings change, you can save tremendous amounts of money by simply "shuffling paper."

ARE YOU OVERPAYING FOR INSURANCE?

People are very familiar with insurance, whether it's life insurance, long-term care, disability, or property and casualty insurance that covers your home, auto, and personal property (like jewelry and art) that you might list. But what is insurance, really? In life, we decide that there are risks that we are willing to be responsible for ourselves, but there are others that we're not willing to gamble on. For instance, I might decide that I'm not going to get long-term care insurance, because my family has good genes and tend to live long and healthy lives. Thus I'm willing to assume the (hopefully small) risk that the same won't be true for me. But I'm not willing to assume the risk for replacing my house if it burns down or if a client slips and falls in my hallway. In buying insurance, we're effectively hiring a third party to assume that risk: the at-fault insurance company.

As a person of wealth, you're going to accrue assets: art, jewelry, wine, and cars. All of these things might need to be insured. But you also need to be insured on your real estate holdings. All of your property insurance coverage needs to be reviewed, especially if they're in multiple states, to see that you're protected properly, to potentially enhance your protection, and to be sure that you're not paying more than you need to be.

One of our clients owns multiple homes and has multiple insurance policies. He had one property in the Massachusetts area where they had damage one year, and he filed a claim. He didn't realize that the insurance company had raised the insurance on that property from $4,000 a year to $18,000 a year because of that claim and additional jewelry and art he had bought. His assistant handles all of his bills, and it wasn't that person's job to pay attention to this kind of thing. But it was our job, so we had a property casualty review done on that. We found a new insurance company that came in and enhanced the coverage of that property while also returning the rate to about $4,000 a year. We saved him $14,000 a year just by looking at what he was paying.

When was the last time that you heard from your property and casualty insurance agent? I'm betting never. When was the last time that you had your coverage on your property reviewed? If you hadn't heard from your agent or haven't reviewed your coverage and costs in the last year or two, you should have this done.

Listed property like artwork and jewelry is normally covered in your home policy, and usually they are individually covered. This is a very lucrative area for insurance companies, and they normally charge higher rates for this type of coverage. Upon annual renewal, insurance companies just add another 10 percent or 15 percent increase a year to all this and keep on raising these rates, whether these items rise in value or not. Again, it's another area to scrutinize, especially if you have a lot of art.

One coverage area that is normally the least costly type of insurance and that sometimes people don't keep up with or don't have at all is personal liability insurance. Personal liability insurance protects you from your negligent acts worldwide. If someone falls down a flight of steps in your home, is injured, and sues you, personal liability insurance covers that. If you're in a shopping mall halfway around the world and you accidentally bump someone who falls down the escalator and they sue you because they have serious injuries, you are protected by having this insurance. You probably already have some personal liability coverage insurance built into your home and auto policies, but you want to add additional personal liability insurance because those other policies sometimes only cover you for half a million or a million dollars. Even though these are events you're unlikely to experience, you could be sued for millions of dollars for a simple accident. You want to make sure that you're covered for that—the good news here is that these policies are very, very inexpensive.

I once advised a client who had his own consulting business and did not have this coverage to get it, and he did, after some procrastination. Not two months later, he was involved in a car accident where he hit a car that had stopped suddenly ahead of him. He was only going fifteen miles per hour. It would have been a minor fender bender, except that the passenger in the car he hit was a very frail, elderly woman. The jolt snapped her head back, and she had to be rushed to the hospital, where she spent three or four months before she passed away—all because of that simple accident. It was a very unusual, catastrophic event.

When he was served with the resulting multimillion-dollar lawsuit from the family and hospital, he called me up in a panic and said, "What do I do?"

I told him, "Just call the insurance company, and they will handle everything for you. You are protected totally from the damage and attorneys' fees." Ever since, he's been my poster child for making sure my clients have personal liability insurance. He's the only one of my clients who has ever had to use it, but it preserved his wealth.

Nobody enjoys contemplating worst-case scenarios, but even so, another important piece of your contingency planning should be life insurance. Life insurance is initially bought to fill gaps in your wealth. If it's important to you to leave behind enough wealth for your loved ones to live the life you wish for them in the event of your death, you get this coverage. When that gap doesn't exist anymore, you might decide that you no longer need life insurance.

But before making that choice and as part of your financial plan, you should explore what life insurance can do as another asset class that allows your money and wealth to grow tax-free. It can also be instrumental in your estate planning, including helping your heirs to avoid paying estate taxes or in creating a legacy for your family, such as a college or charity.

Perhaps you wish to leave a scholarship to a college or an endowment to an art museum. Or you want to fund a trust for your grandchildren and great-grandchildren to make sure they're all educated. Life insurance can be used for any of those purposes, and the process is not complex. I've even shown clients how life insurance can be used to create a secure, future, tax-free stream of income that I have referred to sometimes as a "proxy pension plan." This can be a great way to create more investable cash, tax-free.

Finally, review your healthcare, long-term disability, and long-term care coverages. While these policies can protect your wealth, you might find some opportunities to save investable cash.

PUT ON YOUR OXYGEN MASK FIRST

One common use for investable cash is a very personal choice: the education of your children. Most look at setting up a 529 plan or an account under the Uniform Gifts to Minors Act (UGMA) for their children to save for education. If you're in this group, you may want to consider what we call the "airline rule."

On a flight, you are told that in the event the oxygen masks drop down, you should put yours on first before assisting your child. If you can take care of yourself first, then both you and the child will be okay. We feel the same way when it comes to putting aside wealth for education. If you take care of yourself first, they will be fine. We think that's especially true when it comes to an UGMA. At first, you start to put wealth away in the account, and you are the trustee. Because of the cost of college, these accounts can get into the hundreds of thousands of dollars.

But what happens when your child turns eighteen? When they attain their "majority" age, they're now empowered to run their own affairs. That means that if you've poured money into an UGMA for a child's education, when they turn eighteen, they can decide to use that wealth any way they wish—maybe to "ponder life" for a few years on the beaches of Malibu. If you put the money into a 529 plan, you have more control, but the rate of return is poor on most of these accounts, and fees can be high. If instead you accumulate wealth and add more wealth to what you have, you're going to control how it's spent, hit geometric compounding sooner, achieve your financial plan sooner, and be able to take care of your children.

Not everyone agrees with this philosophically, and that's okay. You make the decisions. Just remember that we're out to make sure you're taken care of first.

You can see that there are myriad ways in which you can find new cash flow without adding to your work hours or years of work life or suffering any lifestyle deprivation, simply by making better and smarter choices in different areas of your financial life. I've just covered a few here; there are many, many more. Be creative! Taking the time to sit down with a good personal financial planner who will give you a structure to look at all these variables annually is probably well worth the time, effort, and money. A good wealth advisor will help you with this—and with the creation of an overall financial plan based on your long-term investment return objective, which we'll discuss in the next chapter.

CHAPTER TEN

WHAT BEING A SAVVY INVESTOR REALLY MEANS— KNOWING YOUR LONG-TERM INVESTMENT RETURN OBJECTIVE

Investing should be more like watching paint dry or watching grass grow. If you want excitement, take $800 and go to Las Vegas.
—Paul Samuelson

Why is having a good investment plan so important? The obvious reason is that people want to have a healthy and safe return on their money. How do most people invest? People love to talk about their investments when they really hit a home run, which is why at a cocktail party, you're likely to hear something like, "I invested in Apple stock many years ago. I've earned 300 percent or 400 percent." You never hear people talk about when they invested in something that didn't turn out as well. But whether they've done well or not is not the real issue. The one thing you might want to ask them is, "What is your long-term investment return objective?" Whenever I ask that, I find that most just stare at me blankly. "What do you mean?"

Sometimes they'll offer some general answers, but when I press the question—what percent return do they "need" to achieve their wealth-building and cash-flow goals?—they cannot tell me. When Apple executives invest in developing a product, they're looking for a return on equity for their shareholders, and they have multiple options of products to choose from to develop. But whatever they choose, there's a long-term investment return objective they are aiming for to make the overall return they feel they need for their shareholders.

I worked for Merck & Co. Inc. As a well-run company, when they were looking at producing a new drug, Merck had a "portfolio" of choices. Their portfolio was the array of drugs they could choose to produce. I remember once touring a factory where the production of a drug was to start. All of a sudden, the production was halted. That factory was gutted, and its equipment was replaced with tens of millions of dollars of new equipment to produce something else. I remember thinking to myself, "Wow, what a waste."

It wasn't until I thought about it more deeply that I realized that it wasn't a waste; they'd made a choice to make another investment that they believed would be far more profitable in their product portfolio, that would have the greatest probability of achieving their long-term investment rate objective or the rate of return they were targeting of their own Wealth Building Formula®. It's the same process when you are looking at the *% Return* of your Wealth Building Formula® and the investment choices in your investment portfolio. Most just look at beating the S&P 500 or the Dow or some other index in a given time period. If they beat them in the latest quarter, they're happy. If they didn't, they're unhappy—but that is not a long-term investment return objective. A long-term investment return objective is about what the rate of return is—on the average, over a long time period with ups and downs in the market—that's going to make your plan work and the probability that your wealth and eventual cash flow needs are achievable at the least possible risk.

OUR INVESTMENT PHILOSOPHY, APPROACH, AND METHODOLOGY

You want to be dealing with investment advisors who have a sound philosophy, approach, and methodology. According to our philosophy, you should do these things:

- Set a reasonably attainable investment return objective.
- Let compounding play a key role in growing your wealth. Let the investment cash remain in place for a long time to allow the power of compounding to become a significant contributor to your wealth accumulation.
- Invest for the long term. A lot of people say they're long-term investors, but when the market dips in a correction or has a crash, you see them making kneejerk reactions. Investing for the long term means not changing course because of short-term fluctuations in the market. Don't chase investment fads.
- Don't try to be a market timer. Nobody has succeeded in second-guessing timing around market fluctuations.
- Only make investments that allow you to sleep well at night. Make sure you know what your advisor's doing, and be well informed about those choices.

Base your portfolio asset allocation decisions and investment selections on what you need in the Wealth Building Formula® of your personal financial plan to either accumulate the wealth you want or add to it and to do so at the least possible risk.

Your personal philosophy may be different; your advisor's may, too, but at least make sure that they have one and you understand it.

WHAT'S YOUR ADVISOR'S APPROACH?

What kind of approach do they take to investing? How do they set about actually investing? Our approach follows the Modern Portfolio Theory (MPT). MPT was created by Harry Markowitz, a Nobel Prize-winning economist, in his paper "Portfolio Selection." It is an investment theory based on the idea that risk-averse investors can create investment portfolios to optimize or maximize expected return based on a given level of market risk. It is one of the most important and influential economic theories dealing with finance and investment of its time.

MPT essentially says that it is possible to construct an optimal investment portfolio that offers the best possible expected return for a given level of risk. By investing in various asset classes like stocks and bonds, you can take advantage of diversification, which reduces the riskiness of the portfolio. You reduce risk by not putting all of your eggs in one investment "basket."

WHAT IS YOUR ADVISOR'S METHODOLOGY?

What procedures or processes do they have for money manager selection? For example, when we select money or fund managers, we look for those who deliver good performance over the long term, have a below-average risk profile for their style of investing, and stay consistent in their investing approach. We have processes and procedures in place to accomplish this.

This isn't meant to be an investment selection book; one could write volumes on that topic alone. That said, I do wish to offer you a process by which to select an investment advisor.

The most important considerations in selecting an investment advisor are their philosophy, approach, and methodology. Your financial planner should first determine your Wealth Building Formula®, which will tell you the long-term investment return objective required from your investment portfolio to achieve your wealth-building, wealth-preservation, and cash-flow requirements.

RISK AND RETURN

Are you comfortable with and willing to accept certain degrees of investment risk required to seek to achieve the investment rate of return you need? If you're not, then lower the rate of return until you are. This is what is discussed with your investment advisor and/or wealth advisor (which can be the same person, assuming they are properly qualified). If you have a Wealth Building Formula®, you know that if you increase the *% Return*, then the other variables like *T* (time) and *C* (investable cash) will decrease. You will achieve what you wish in less time and with less wealth. Or, on the right side of the equation, you will have more *$$$* (cash flow). Knowing your risk tolerance (how you feel about possible decreases in value of your portfolio) is important to sleeping well at night.

In earlier chapters I've written about how finding investable cash can reduce the necessary risk in your portfolio. As a simple example, suppose that you have a $5 million investment portfolio and you determine by your Wealth Building Formula® that your *% Return* or your long-term investment return objective should be 6 percent. However, you find a way to generate additional investable cash of $50,000 per year through our Integrated Cash Flow Management℠ process. One percent of $5 million is $50,000. Since you have found this additional cash flow, you may be able to reduce your *% Return* to 5 percent instead of 6 percent, thus lowering the risk in your investment portfolio. If you want more cash flow from your wealth, and you cannot find more investable cash elsewhere, then the return you receive from your portfolio has to increase, which will increase your risk.

By determining the cash flow required in your financial plan, you're going to determine what the return target is that you need to hit for your portfolio. Then you can make an informed investment decision based on that and how you wish to invest your money. The higher the rate of return you choose, the greater the risk you assume. The lower the rate of return you choose, the less risk is involved. If you are a person who does not like a lot of risk, then you might choose a lower rate of return. Therefore, finding more investable cash and opportunities will allow you to add more to your wealth. This will give you the choice of less risk to achieve your financial plan and the cash flow you need to achieve financial independence or, if independent, to grow new wealth and increase your cash flow.

THE TRAUST SOLLUS WAY OF THINKING

Our philosophy, approach, and methodology are aimed at ensuring that you are going to have the highest probability of achieving the long-term investment return objective or *% Return* you require for your financial plan, at the lowest possible risk. We believe in MPT and that a highly diversified portfolio is the least risky and best choice. You, along with your advisor, need to actively monitor the performance of your portfolio; your advisor is responsible for reporting clearly and accurately to you the gross and net investment performance of all management fees.

A sophisticated yet straightforward approach to investing is best. Wealth building is a journey that goes smoothest when you know both your destination and when you'd like to arrive there—the amount that you're building toward and the number of years you have to get there. Once a clear destination and desired time frame are established, you can effectively develop and manage an investment portfolio that is focused on achieving your specific goals. Sophisticated institutional investors understand this; that's why their approach to investing is to include portfolio holdings designed to generate, over the long term, the average annual return required to reach their goal within the planned time frame. Most individual investors err by not first taking these steps. As a result, many of them become overly preoccupied with building a portfolio that they feel will generate a return exceeding that of the S&P 500 index.

HOW WE MEASURE SUCCESS

We believe that the correct way to measure success in wealth building is to gauge whether you remain on track to reaching your desired wealth goal in the planned time period, not the actual average annual rate of return you achieve. Sophisticated investors recognize that anything else is just a distraction. Perhaps you have a goal of earning 6 percent a year; there will be years you're going to be above that and years you'll be below it. What matters is that you are achieving your financial plan at the least possible risk.

When you're looking for an investment advisor, we suggest an independent, registered investment advisor (RIA). That means that you want a professional who is only going to make decisions in your best interests. If you are not using an RIA, you are most likely using a broker. Brokers aren't held to as high a fiduciary standard. If you want to get unbiased advice based on what is in your best interests, always choose an independent RIA, especially one who finds money managers or funds for you and does not offer proprietary funds (ones they own) or receives any compensation from a money manager. The only fee your advisor should be receiving is from you.

PASSIVE VERSUS ACTIVE MANAGEMENT

While this is not a book on investing, we should talk a little about another aspect of investment approach: passive versus active investment management. Passive management is usually investing in index funds. You invest money in an index fund, which follows the market of that fund. It is normally low cost and relatively easy to do but can result in higher taxes, and risk can also be higher. Due to just achieving the index return, when fees are deducted, it can result in you always underperforming the index. Also, you still have to decide on asset classes, allocation, and rebalancing the allocation to manage risk.

An active management approach means that your advisor selects managers who buy and sell securities based on their analyses and do not just follow an index. An advisor may also select individual securities. While their performance may be compared to an index, they will perform differently than the index. They may perform higher or lower, but you do have the chance to outperform the index. Fees are normally higher. It can be more complicated, but tax efficiency is better, and risk can be managed more effectively.

The ongoing debate is which management style performs better over time. Passive tends to be a better performer in rapidly rising markets, while active tends to perform better in a more volatile market. Over the long term, they tend to perform the same. We at Traust Sollus believe that there are good points in both ways of investing, and we advocate having a blend.

There are certain parts of the market where it's better to have a passive investment or an index approach because of the cost or there not being much opportunity in that part of the market. This is normally in large company stocks or international markets. We think that when it comes to smaller companies, it is much better to have individual securities because there are more and greater opportunities for active managers.

We've seen investment advisors who are proponents of passive investing, but they don't really talk about risk. To us, risk management is a necessary component of managing a portfolio. We find that there are more opportunities to save tax dollars with an actively managed portfolio. In our portfolio management, we use technology to watch how active managers buy and sell. By watching and employing software, we have been able to add as little as a fraction of a percent up to 2 percent or more annually to the return of a portfolio.

There are other advantages for active management: executives who work for large companies may have a concentrated holding in the securities of their own company and don't want any more in that particular company or industry. Active management can avoid adding those securities, whereas you would have to accept them as part of the holdings in an index fund. We've had clients who, for either religious reasons or on principle, don't want to be invested in what we call the "sin stocks": tobacco, gambling, or alcohol. We can remove those from a portfolio, which again is normally impossible when you're buying into non-specific index funds. Other clients have environmental or political concerns and don't want to invest in companies they feel violate their principles.

ASK ABOUT THE REPORTING PROCESS

When interviewing your potential investment advisor or talking with the one you already have, make sure that you clearly understand the reports on performance you receive. As President Reagan once replied when asked about trusting a foe with a treaty, "Trust, but verify." Verification ensures that you are on track with your Wealth Building Formula® and your financial plan and that your investments are earning the *% Return* you need. You should receive, at the very least, a quarterly report on your portfolio that allows you to track what your rate of return has been for that particular quarter, year to date, and since inception in absolute dollars, gross and net of management fees. Performance should also be reported as a percentage, also before and after management fees. That allows you to see what you have actually earned.

Too many brokerage houses and managers issue reports that are confusing or do not provide that amount of detail. That makes it tough to know if you're on track with your Wealth Building Formula® or are on the right path to achieving your goals. By the way, it's not because they can't do this; the technology is there. These companies simply don't want to have to disclose all their fees and fee arrangements to you. You should demand this; it's what a well-run company would do, and your aim should be to run your personal finances in the same fashion. Demand accountability and clear documentation.

Your actual *% Return*, in part, is going to determine how long you have to work, how much wealth you have, and the cash flow that can be produced from that wealth. It will determine what level of risk you might have to take. As I laid out in the ground rules, it's up to you to decide how involved in the process you wish to be. But if you're not paying attention, be prepared to make do with whatever the market produces for you—not what you could have produced.

So far, we've talked chiefly about building wealth. Now we're going to switch gears and discuss how to protect it for your loved ones or future generations.

CHAPTER ELEVEN

ESTATE PLANNING— PROTECTING WHAT YOU HAVE BUILT

Good fortune is what happens when
opportunity meets with planning.
—Thomas Alva Edison

Whether through your own diligent efforts, inheritance, or the lottery, you have wealth—and hopefully more wealth than you'll need or want to spend in your life. What do you want to accomplish with your money, now or beyond your lifetime?

WHAT KIND OF LEGACY DO YOU WISH TO LEAVE?

Perhaps you want to be sure that in the event of your passing, your spouse is secure in the same lifestyle you're enjoying together now or that your other loved ones—children and grandchildren—will have the opportunities in life that money can provide.

You may wish to accomplish something else with your money, such as giving it to charity or a school. However, if you don't put together a will or the other estate-planning documents that establish your wishes legally, the people who will likely determine what happens to your money will be your state government or the courts. Estate planning is also a way to preserve wealth and cash flow from avoidable taxation.

There are some real horror stories out there about people who should have been savvy enough to have planned adequately for their estates but failed to do so. When the heir to the Wrigley chewing gum fortune died some years ago, his estate planning was so deficient that his estate paid tens of millions of dollars to the government. The family had owned the Chicago Cubs for generations, but because of this planning failure, they had to sell the team to pay their tax bills. Experts who reviewed their estate documents subsequently said that this catastrophe was completely avoidable. Keep in mind that we're not talking about adding wealth at this point; we're looking at strategies to preserve your wealth for your loved ones and for generations beyond that. If you don't have any family or any desire to contribute to society beyond your lifetime, and you do have a strong desire to hand your estate over to Uncle Sam, you can skip this chapter—but most of us do care about what we leave behind.

THE DOCUMENTS YOU MUST HAVE AND SHOULD HAVE

The first document you want in an adequate estate plan is a will. A properly written will can accomplish a few basic wishes for you. First, you will determine who will be in charge of seeing that your wishes, as expressed in your will, are carried out. That's your executor. Second, you're going to determine how you wish your estate to be distributed. If you have minor children, you're going to determine who you would like to act as guardians if you pass away before they've reached majority age.

A will is the primary estate instrument, but there are other documents you should have in order as well, depending on your circumstances. You might create what is called an irrevocable life insurance trust (ILIT). Placing life insurance in a trust will save estate taxes. In any case, you should have a medical care directive or a living will. This will direct your medical care when you are unable to make those decisions. You might also consider other documents, like a limited power of attorney or a durable power of attorney. These documents allow trusted people you select to make decisions for you if you are unable to do so for yourself. Various types of trusts can also be established during your lifetime or upon your passing that can fulfill your intentions and ensure that the government receives the least amount of taxes possible. Without these crucial documents in place, the government could step in and decide what is best for you or your loved ones and who gets your hard-earned money.

A limited power of attorney or a durable power of attorney comes into play in a situation in which you are temporarily incapacitated but are expected to recover. I had a client once, an attorney, who resisted doing this; within weeks after he finally got this document done, he was in a car accident with his wife that left them both hospitalized, and they could not manage their financial affairs. They could not sign checks. They could not conduct certain business transactions. A limited power of attorney will give the people who you designate the power to write checks or do limited transactions for you as you recover.

A durable power of attorney is broader, granting the person named the rights to do more extensive financial chores for you. Most people want a limited power of attorney because they want the designee to be able to handle their affairs, but they don't want them to be empowered to sell their home or make similar major decisions for which they'd want to give consent.

Estate planning is an important part of your comprehensive personal financial plan. As part of our work with clients, we review every aspect of estate planning and advise where action should be taken to make sure your estate is in good order, down to what kinds of insurance you have. We do this either to make sure your loved ones are taken care of and other legacy wishes are accomplished, or once you have exhausted every possible means of sheltering your estate, to pay whatever kind of estate taxes that you might owe.

NOBODY WANTS TO THINK ABOUT IT

Quite frankly, we find that for most people, estate planning is the last on the list of things to do. Maybe they don't want to admit to themselves that they're going to die or to make decisions about who gets what or who's going to be in charge. But honestly, that's a little selfish when you stop to consider the burden this places on your spouse, siblings, parents, or friends. Will they step in to help? Will anyone know what to do? Yet most people spend more time selecting the toppings to order on a pizza than thinking about planning for their estate. Many who have spent the time to establish a simple will may find that it's not adequate to preserve the wealth they have built during their lives or to protect their loved ones in the event of sudden death. You may assume that your spouse can handle it all, but what if you're in an accident and your spouse is with you? It may not be enough just to rely on a will.

TAXES AND TRUSTS

When people think about what they want to have happen to their wealth when they pass, they nearly always want to avoid taxes. They also wish to have some control. In order to accomplish those aims, you might consider establishing trusts. This may allow you to take advantage of the exemptions the government gives to you and allow that wealth to continue to grow outside of your estate, avoiding estate taxes. As mentioned earlier, placing your life insurance into an ILIT allows you to determine where you want the funds to go and also removes it from your estate and taxation.

You may explore other types of trusts to set up; one type to consider is called a spousal lifetime access trust (SLAT). This allows you to put the federal exemption amount for you and your spouse into a trust. As of this writing, this is a little more than $5 million per spouse. This allows that money to grow free of estate tax, out of your estate and to future generations. A great feature of these particular trusts is that both spouses can have access to the funds during their lifetimes, if needed.

Another instrument is a grantor retained annuity trust (GRAT). This trust allows you to put assets in now and to receive income from these assets for a certain period as an annual payment from the trust. When you pass, any assets remaining will be turned over to your beneficiary—usually a close family member—as a gift.

Another strategy is called a qualified terminable interest property (QTIP). It's meant to take advantage of a marital deduction to control the ultimate distribution of assets after the death of both spouses. Simply, for estate purposes, any property that passes to a current spouse is not subject to gift or estate tax. However, the whole property must pass to the current spouse. The transfer through a QTIP is an exception, as long as the current spouse has lifetime interest in the property. QTIPs are commonly used when a spouse has children from another marriage. The spouse bringing the property into the marriage may wish to provide for this new spouse for their lifetime and take advantage of their unified tax credit but nonetheless designate where the money goes after the new spouse is deceased. A QTIP allows this to be accomplished.

All of these are complex instruments that change all of the time. Depending on your specific situation, there could be many options to explore. Knowing which best serves your needs is most soundly decided by working with a very knowledgeable wealth advisor or estate-planning attorney. I would strongly advise against just using websites like LegalZoom.com for your estate planning.

Lastly, some words of advice: Don't be in a hurry to give away your estate. Make sure you have assets that generate the cash flow you need for your lifetime. I knew of a situation in which a very wealthy couple transferred assets to trusts for their children. Due to unforeseen circumstances, the children wound up with great wealth, while the parents' wealth decreased drastically and left them dependent on the children. It's important to make sure that you have experts working with you to help you sort through the ramifications of your choices and to tell you what you need to prepare. As in all cases when using an expert, make sure they are of "championship" caliber.

CHAPTER TWELVE

CREATING A
CHAMPIONSHIP TEAM

*Achieving the lifestyle you want now and in the future
is a lot easier when you surround yourself with a
championship-caliber team of experts.*
—Albert J. Zdenek Jr.

I f you read only one chapter in this book, I hope it's this one.

You make financial choices each day, and there are experts that you depend on for prudent advice and guidance. It's critical that these experts know what the plan is: What lifestyle do you wish to lead, now and in the future? What are your values? What is important to you? If your advisors do not know these answers, they will not be able to steer you in the right direction, no matter their level of expertise. Your current accountant, attorney, banker, insurance agent, pension expert, and others may not know you or may not be working together as they should be to obtain the best results for you. They could be individual players, playing their own games, making decisions based on what they do for everyone else rather than what the game plan is for you—what you need.

YOU DON'T NEED TO BE AN EXPERT

You do not need to become a CPA, attorney, or any sort of expert yourself. However, the better you select the "players" on your team—a team that knows the overall game plan and has been tailored to your needs—the better financial choices you'll be able to make and the better chance you'll have to achieve the wealth and cash flow you need to live the life you want, now and forever.

How should your team of experts work? I use the Yankees as an example, even though I'm a Phillies fan. When George Steinbrenner was the owner of the Yankees, they were in the playoffs or in contention almost every year. Many times they were world champions. Steinbrenner made sure that the very best players were on that team in their proper positions. Having the best players always guaranteed that the team was going to be competitive. Look to building your expert team with the same idea.

Most of us are far less intentional when we build our teams; they just seem to happen. We get out of school and get a car, so we get car insurance. We probably use the agent our parents used or a college buddy who's selling insurance. As needs arise, we add other players, but we don't look at changing the ones we have, as our needs become more complicated or demand more sophistication. The Phillies had some good years too but not consistently. They struggle most years. Do you find yourselves struggling to get things done?

If you build yourself a championship team of experts, you have the best chance of achieving what you want. Anything less, lessens that likelihood. Anything less could mean that you work longer and harder in life, that you make poor financial choices, and that you and your loved ones may not live the way you wish.

HOW DO YOU KNOW YOU HAVE CHAMPIONSHIP TEAM PLAYERS?

You may never know how much knowledge an expert has, but you can see the way the experts and their staff treat you. Do they return your phone calls in a timely fashion? When they promise to complete work in a certain time frame, do they do so? Or are they always late, requiring you to call them? When you're dealing with their staff, whether it's their receptionist or the people who assist them, are you being treated with friendly, high-touch service? Do they care about important events in your life? Do they know the names of your children? Is your expert proactive? Do they call you once in a while, not because you called them but because they thought of an idea for you?

Note that I have not discussed whether they are competent professionals. Most championship sports teams do not have superstars at all positions. Some have none. But good team members show diligent work ethics and respect for other team members, and they pull together to win. The main way you can judge your experts is by how you are treated by them and their staff. If you are not getting proactive service, promptly returned calls, or work completed properly and on time, maybe you're not getting the best services.

You have a choice. You can change players, or instead of having an A team, you can keep your B or C team players. If you have B team players, you'll have a B team financial plan, you'll have B team financial help or guidance, and there's a greater chance that you're going to work longer in life, you're not going to have as much as you should have, and you're not going to live the life you wish. If you have an A team, it's more likely that you're going to build what you want in life, you're going to live life the way you want, and you're going to be able to accomplish what you want.

THE ROLE OF THE WEALTH ADVISOR

You are the team owner. You pay them, and they do what you want. You create the plan to "win the championship" (your financial plan) with the "coach" you hire (your wealth advisor). We review the experts that work with our clients. If we see a B or C player, we let our clients know. If we get any comment from a client other than, "They're terrific," we tell them that it may be time to look around for someone else. It's a big red flag when a person says, "Well, Joe's been my insurance agent since I got out of college twenty-five years ago, and he's a good old boy," or anything like that. Our question is, "Okay, what has Joe done for you recently?" We find out that the only time he's in contact with Joe, besides going golfing or fishing, is when he thinks of a need and he calls Joe.

Reality check: if you're coming up with or reading about better ideas than are the people on your expert list, you'd better start to replace them. If you have your own business, you know that you have some A, B, and C players as employees. The surest road to ruin for a business is to have C players on the payroll. B employees may not be that much better. When it comes to your team of experts, if you don't have all A players, you're not going to be able to accomplish what you could have, and it's going to be a longer struggle for you.

Having a championship team in place helps our clients make the best financial decisions for themselves, build and preserve the wealth they need, and manage it more effectively. As a result, they sleep better at night than those people who have a subpar team. During times of emergency or uncertainty, this is even more important. When the market's not doing well or things are going wrong in your life—if there's an unexpected death or an illness, you lose your job, or your business is going through terrible times—a championship team is an invaluable asset. Don't let sentiment, habit, or being busy keep you from assembling the best team you possibly can. Your financial life and those of your loves ones literally depend on it.

IN CLOSING...

I feel that luck is preparation meeting opportunity.
—Oprah Winfrey

I have been very fortunate to meet people in my life who allowed me the opportunity to transform my life and to live as I wish. I hope that reading this book has inspired you to begin to construct your life the way you wish, now and in the future. Sometimes, the first steps to transform your life are the most difficult.

If you are ready to transform your financial life and want to take those steps, please contact me and my team at Traust Sollus Wealth Management, LLC. We get up every day to transform the lives of our clients, family, and friends. We would be privileged to help you transform yours.

We Transform Lives

CONTACT INFORMATION

AL ZDENEK

President & CEO
Traust Sollus Wealth Management, LLC
70 East 55th Street, 12th Floor
New York, New York 10023
212-661-8682
AZdenek@TSWealth.com

ABOUT THE AUTHOR

AL ZDENEK

A l Zdenek is the president, chief executive officer, and founder of Traust Sollus. Al is a certified public accountant (CPA) and a personal financial specialist (PFS). He has over thirty years' experience in transforming the lives of people, guiding them to make better financial choices to achieve the way they wish to live now and in the future. He does this through his company, providing wealth management services to high-net worth individuals, senior executives, physicians, and business owners. Al's work with clients includes comprehensive personal financial planning, investment portfolio construc-

tion and management, analysis of and ongoing strategic support for both personal and business-related cash flow management, tax planning and preparation, retirement planning, trust and estate planning, planned giving, and sophisticated life insurance strategies.

Over the years, Al has been among those selected to appear in lists of the nation's top financial advisors and is often quoted in the media about wealth building and wealth management topics. He has authored many articles on wealth management issues that concern and affect the types of clients Traust Sollus serves.

Al has been invited to present on wealth management topics to many senior executive and professional association meetings across the country, including many corporate meetings, the National Association of Personal Financial Advisors (NAPFA), the American Institute of Certified Public Accountants (AICPA), many state societies of CPAs, the American Gastroenterological Association, the Healthcare Financial Management Association, and many medical institutions. He has served on the board of directors of Somerset Medical Center, Somerville, NJ. He also is a prominent speaker at conferences for wealth management industry professionals, leading teaching sessions on firm management topics such as mergers and acquisitions, firm vision, managing firm goals, and succession planning.

His public service includes being elected for nine years to the Borough of Flemington Council, Flemington, NJ. His duties included serving seven years as police commissioner of the borough. Prior to founding the company he was employed by Arthur Young & Co., NYC and Merck & Co., Inc.

He holds a BA from Rutgers College and an MBA degree from Rutgers Graduate School of Business. Al is listed in the International Who's Who of Entrepreneurs. Al's hobbies include traveling internationally, wine, cooking, reading, and collecting art. He also spends time supporting the Inner-City Scholarship Fund of New York City, Virtual Enterprises Inc., and other charities and teaching.

He lives in Manhattan and Paris.